# T[]
# SECRET [] []
# []C
# MASONIC
# INITIATION

Robert Lomas

www.robertlomas.com
www.bradford.ac.uk/webofhiram/
www.knight-lomas.com

Lewis Masonic

Dedicated to

A LEWIS

on his Initiation

*Xelyth*

## Designer Masonic Jewellery
### Makers of The Hiram Key Pin
### www.DelythUK.com

The Secret Science of Masonic Initiation
Robert Lomas

First published 2008

ISBN 978 0 85318 318 1

Published by Lewis Masonic an imprint of Ian Allan Publishing Ltd,
Hersham, Surrey KT12 4RG.

Printed in England by Ian Allan Printing Ltd, Hersham, Surrey KT12 4RG.

Visit the Lewis Masonic website at www.lewismasonic.com

# ACKNOWLEDGMENTS

I would like to thank two people for inspiring me to write this book. The first is Brother Martin Jackson, a master craftsman in the art of Tracing Boards, who has spent many hours probing my emotional response to Freemasonry. Martin forced me to articulate ideas that I felt but never tried to put into words. The second is Mark Booth, one of the best editors it has ever been my good fortune to work with. Under the pen-name of Jonathan Black, Mark wrote a book called *The Secret History of the World as Laid Down by the Secret Societies*. In it he demonstrated a writing technique that suggested a way for me to answer Bro Martin's questions in the spirit they were asked, whilst remaining true to my scientific values.

In the opening of *The Secret History* Mark wrote:

> This is a history of the world that has been taught down the ages in certain secret societies. It may seem quite mad from today's point of view, but an extraordinarily high proportion of men and women who made history have been believers ...
> I am asking readers to approach this text in a new way – to see it as an imaginative exercise. I want the reader to try to imagine what it would feel like to believe the opposite of what we have been brought up to believe.

These few sentences inspired me to step back from the scientific position I usually adopt and write a book that makes a similar request. I ask my readers to temporarily set aside science and to listen, as a child, to the ancient teaching of the Craft as it shows you how you might know yourself. This book will take you on an imaginative journey deep into that inner part of your consciousness that Freemasonry calls your soul.

I would also like to thank Jonathan Black for his

stimulating discussion and for generously contributing a foreword to this little volume of imagination.

The Solomon Lodge of Research No. 5986 in Saskatchewan and Bro Heath Armbruster kindly volunteered to be Masonic guinea-pigs for my venture into a different writing style by respectively reading, and listening to, some to the key chapters in early draft and then discussing them before commenting on their substance. Thank you, Brethren, for your indulgence.

I thank John Wheelwright for applying his excellent copy-editing skills and good humour to sorting out my manuscript, spotting my exercises in creative spelling and tidying up my layouts.

I thank Martin Faulks and Nick Grant at Lewis Masonic for agreeing to publish my musings, and Bill Hamilton and Corrine Charbet, my agents at A.M. Heath, for sorting out the practical details.

Finally I want to thank my wife and children for their continuing support.

Also by Robert Lomas

*Turning the Hiram Key*
*Turning the Solomon Key*
*Turning the Templar Key*
*The Secrets of Freemasonry*
*The Invisible College*
*The Man Who Invented the Twentieth Century*
*Freemasonry and the Birth of Modern Science*

With Chris Knight

*The Hiram Key*
*The Second Messiah*
*Uriel's Machine*
*The Book of Hiram*

With Geoffrey Lancaster

*Forecasting for Sales and Material Management*

# TABLE OF CONTENTS

# FOREWORD

by Jonathan Black

Any collector develops a nose for 'the real thing', and as someone who has spent many years seeking out revealing literature on the subject of initiation I felt assured as soon as I began to read this book that the author knows what he is talking about.

I met Robert Lomas many years ago when I edited and published his first bestseller, which he wrote with Christopher Knight, called *The Hiram Key*. It was a manuscript with a helter-skelter pace and charged with the excitement of making dizzying discoveries and seeing old worlds in new ways. The opening of this new book announces a deep and solemn change in Robert Lomas as a writer and as a man. Something has happened to him.

The enemies of Freemasonry like to see it as a club for men who seek unfair material advantages. Of course it may be the case – who knows? – that some individuals hope for this. But Robert Lomas reveals how the rites and symbolism of Freemasonry are intended to awake, perhaps gently and over time, sometimes suddenly and decisively, any spiritual curiosity, any curiosity about esoteric mysteries that lies inside the individual, however deep, however dormant. New dimensions may open up to him.

This short book contains as clear an account as I have ever read of the gifts and benefits that initiation brings. In my own book, *The Secret History of the World*, I talked about the way that different schools of initiation have flowed through history – for example, Greek, Roman, Cabalistic and Sufi. They intermingle and evolve, sharing certain essential beliefs and practices, but each – if they are true – addressing the spiritual needs of a particular age and place. It seemed to me that Freemasonry had a historic role to play, beginning with the scientific revolution and, intimately connected with this revolution, the great paradigmatic shift from idealism to materialism. In the seventeenth century physical objects began to become the yardstick of what is real, and spiritual realities, which had seemed blazingly real in earlier ages, began to flicker and fade. In this context the esoteric mission of Freemasonry has been to help lead humanity through an age of great materialism, a new Dark Age, while keeping the flame of true spirituality alive.

Great Freemasonic thinkers have therefore been concerned to work out what we can truly and reasonably say about spiritual matters. They have always been particularly wary of straying into superstition. So it's highly significant, that Robert Lomas is a scientist by training, yet he writes in an explicit way – which some will find surprising – about the continuing life of the spirit apart from the physical body. He alludes, too, to a universal Moral Law, a Divine Plan, to a Masonic astrology, to elements of esoteric physiology – what are called in other schools of thought the *chakras* – and also the various gifts that initiation brings, which, as I point out in my own book, are not un-adjacent to the gifts of the Holy Spirit outlined in the New Testament.

It's significant because these things would seem to sit uneasily with much of mainstream science, though that is not to say that they are not ultimately reconcilable with what scientists may soon come to discover. And that, I think, is the key point – and what makes Robert Lomas such an important writer. As a practising scientist he recognises the value of experiment and experience, and as a scientist and Freemason he also knows the importance of keeping an open mind, of not rushing to impose conventional or established explanations on new data, of not taking a partisan view. He is always alert to new developments in science, dismissing nothing out of hand, no matter how weird or far-fetched they might at first seem. If the rites and meditative practices described in this book work; if, as he knows from repeated personal experience, they reliably produce the changes in consciousness it is claimed they produce, then that is a reason – not necessarily a determining one, but certainly a good reason – for believing they there might ultimately be some truth somewhere in the religious beliefs that gave rise to these practices.

Could it be part of the mission of Freemasonry, one of the many great benefits that it brings to the world, that it will help reconcile idealism and materialism, science and religion? We are setting off on a journey into unknown territory, and I commend

Robert Lomas as a wise and good-hearted guide, in the first instance to the mysteries of Freemasonic initiation. You are standing on the threshold of a revelation that is, to borrow the author's own phrase, 'truly magical'. Initiation is dangerous, even deadly, but what may perhaps be most surprising to the enemies of Freemasonry, is to learn that what is at the heart of it … is love.

JONATHAN BLACK (né MARK BOOTH)

# PREFACE

Once in a while a person is born whose thoughts live on long after their death. One such man, Walter Leslie Wilmshurst, was born on 22 June 1867 in Sussex.

Seventy-two years later, on 19 July 1939, he was hailing a taxi in North London when he collapsed in the street. By the time help reached him he was dead. When he died Brother Wilmshurst left an incredible legacy from his fifty years as a Freemason.

He was a cautious and private man, who took as his motto 'govern the lips, they are the palace doors, and the king is within'. He was a Freemason of his time and didn't speak of his Masonry outside the Lodge. Yet he thought deeply about it and shared his thoughts. He published books, he wrote lectures to deliver to his lodge, he created private teaching materials to help his junior brethren, he held discussions in Lodges of Instruction and kept detailed notebooks of his thoughts.

I have been a student of Wilmshurst for over fifteen years, since I read his book *The Meaning of Masonry*. I found that book interesting but difficult to follow. It was made up of five disparate lectures, originally given as talks in lodges, and did not seem to have been edited into a coherent narrative. Yet it was clear that Bro. Wilmshurst knew much more than he was prepared to write about. He admitted as much when he said:

> In giving these pages to publication care has been taken to
> observe due reticence in respect of essential matters. An
> elementary and formal secrecy is requisite as a practical
> precaution against the intrusion of improper persons and
> for preventing profanation.

Recently I have been looking closely at how Masonic ritual works, and what effect it has on people. As part of that study I did a complete survey of all that Wilmshurst had written on Freemasonry. I looked at his published and unpublished work, his private and public statements, his printed and handwritten writings, and I made a fascinating discovery. There was a scattered thread running through his work.

I realised that, when I combined his unformed thoughts in his notebooks, his private statements in his lodge lectures, his musings in the annotations on the margins of his personal books and the content of his published books, this corpus made up an advanced course in the secret science of Masonry. At first I used my insights to create a series of lodge lectures which started from the question 'Why become a Mason?' and worked through the steps of the Masonic degrees to end up describing what it means to work as a Masonic Initiate within a Lodge.

I have given these lectures many times and received much supportive feedback. But I was still troubled that these ideas, so useful for any brother who wants to make his daily progress in Masonic knowledge, were not available to the Craft in general. So I decided to write a book, specifically for the Masonic fraternity which summed up my understanding of 'The Craft' of Freemasonry and this is it, *The Secret Science of Masonic Initiation*.

What is its purpose? Let me quote the words of my long dead inspirational master to explain what prompted me to write it.

Throughout the ages the aspirant to Initiation has found it essential to pass under the personal tuition of some expert teacher who knows the way and can give him help suited to his personal requirements. Hence the Craft, following this traditional method, declares that every new Apprentice shall find a Master and from him gain instruction. For the opened Lodge was never intended to be a place for instruction; it is a place for corporate realisation of the truths in which we are to be instructed privately elsewhere.

It rests upon not only the moral duty of every more advanced Brother to help the less advanced, but upon the spiritual principle that whoever has freely received must as freely give, that no one is initiated for his private advantage but must pass on his light to someone below him on the life-ladder.

I was first inspired by the thoughts of Walter Wilmshurst, then, as I structured my reflections into a series of self-contained narrative modules, I came to a set of answers to my questions about Masonic Initiation. Perhaps these answers could have some wider appeal, and by writing them down in this volume I might spread knowledge about the inner meaning of Freemasonry to a new generation of Masons. But, I warn you, if you are not yourself a Mason, you will find that much here makes little sense to you. I have set out to inform the Master Mason about the great adventure that Initiation offers; if you do not already know the rituals, you will struggle to follow their reasoning. This book is not an exposé, neither is it a step-by-step guide to make you a Mason. If you want to be made a Mason, then you will need to join a lodge, and there are many lodges, both male and female, that will welcome you if you only ask. Masonry is not a solitary occupation; it is an inspirational ritual practice carried out by groups of consenting adults in private.

Freemasonry offers a system of training the soul. Whether or not you believe in the concept of a soul, the Masonic system works and improves your life. To benefit from Masonic Initiation you must be prepared to accept that you can train your soul (whatever that might be) and that if you do so you will benefit. But questions about the nature of the soul must wait for another time and another place.

Plate 1: The First-Degree Tracing Board
(courtesy of www.tracingboards.com).

Plate 2: The Second-Degree Tracing Board
(courtesy of www.tracingboards.com).

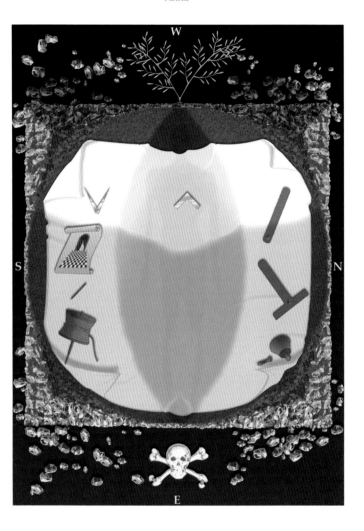

Plate 3: The Third-Degree Tracing Board
(courtesy of www.tracingboards.com).

Plate 4: The Tracing Board of the Centre
(courtesy of www.tracingboards.com).

# CHAPTER ONE

## WHY BECOME A MASON?

Why should you want to become a Freemason?

Freemasonry is not a social or welfare club, although it is sociable and promotes its members' welfare. Nor is it a charitable organisation, although is does act charitably. It is not even a dining club, although its members often dine together.

If it were any of these, or even all of them, its value would be no greater than any other secular clubs. But Freemasonry is not secular. It has a deep purpose, which is often overlooked in the rush of the modern world.

Its secret science is that of knowing yourself; its object is to seek out truth; and its working tools are reason and argument.

It is one of the largest spiritual organisations in the world. Its total membership is vast – so vast it is difficult to estimate a full head count. The idea of Masonry is popular and has taken a firm grip upon many people's imaginations. Differences in race, gender and language have not restricted its spread and popularity.

Yet Masons take the appeal of their strange institution for granted; the spread of the Masonic system throughout the world is something that does not seem to surprise them. But outsiders do wonder what the secret of its worldwide appeal is. This popularity is a problem shared by students of Freemasonry and conspiracy theorists.

Many answers can be put forward to explain why Freemasonry is so popular. Their value often depends on the wit of the person answering, or their degree of sympathy for Masonry.

Is the Craft just a social, fraternal, back-scratching network? Does it simply provide opportunities for creeps, who think themselves a cut above the common herd, to mix on their own perceived level? These are flimsy motives to sustain a well-supported worldwide organisation that has always drawn to itself the movers and shakers of society. George Washington, King George VI and Mozart do not seem to have needed covert Masonic help to boost their careers or prop up their egos.

Perhaps it is a tool for promoting practical charity and human welfare. It certainly does this, and makes quite a good job of it. But Masonry is not a high-grade Friendly Society or a cheap form of mutual insurance provider. Its charitable efforts are a *result* of its existence, not the motive for it.

Is it a school of morality, tending to promote peace and goodwill? It does do that – but why should you need to join an oddball society, or take great vows of secrecy, merely to learn simple ethics?

Are the cynics right? Is Freemasonry an engine to promote the mutual interests of its members and the downfall of non-members? Is it a cover for political intrigue? Is it a screen for propagating anti-religious ideas?

I'm sorry to disappoint you, but it isn't.

In the past Freemasonry has taken part in political plots. I'm sure you will recall the actions of the Jacobites and Legitimists in both England and France in more revolutionary times. And we all recognise the Freemasons of Boston and their infamous Tea Party. So I have to admit there is some truth in the political claim. But, just because certain Freemasons in the past took political action, this does not prove that the Masonic system *itself* has a political purpose. In my view, British Masonry is more innocent of political motive than a Mother's Union meeting. Even Clement XII's notorious (and never rescinded) ban on Roman Catholics becoming Freemasons, or having anything to do with Freemasonry, in his encyclical *In eminenti* of 4 May 1738, was based on a political misunderstanding. (At that time Prime Minister Walpole was using Freemasonry as a political and intelligence tool against the deposed James II, whose cause the Papacy was seeking to promote. So the political motive was Walpole's, not Freemasonry's.)

This leaves few reasons that could explain both the spread and the charm of the Masonic system. But one stands out, at least to those of us who work its Degrees: the power of its ceremonial rites. Are its ritual workings the secret of Masonry's vitality and widespread popularity? I can think of no other reason to explain its success.

For many in our fraternity the voice of ritual is not a loud one, and its import is only dimly felt. But some Masons do realise the intellectual depth of the Craft's heritage. Something veiled, latent and deeply rooted in our rites speaks to something that is latent but responsive in us who take part. Something greater than just the impressiveness and solemnity of the rites remains, unrealised and unformulated, in our consciousness. In us who take part Masonic ritual induces a feeling that we are in the presence of a mystery that goes to the root of our being. And it feels good to go there.

But what is it about Masonic rites that causes this appeal? Is it our communal history?

Many suppose Masonry to be passed down from time immemorial. They think it was instituted, on a whim among ancient inhabitants of the East, and just happens to have been perpetuated in the West. The mythical history, regularly told and retold within the rituals of the Craft, recounts how the forerunners of Freemasonry built the Temple of Israel at Jerusalem whilst working for King Solomon, and we Masons just carry on their traditions.

As a Mason, you know that the Craft claims to initiate you into secrets and mysteries. It's clear that our system uses the tools and terms of working masons as metaphors. But a moment's reflection shows that the secrets and mysteries that are revealed are not those of any industrial trade. Are the mundane activities of the builder's trade being used to hide truths of a moral, or even a spiritual, nature? And then we have to think about the Third Degree. As we stand up in lodge and recite the traditional history, we are retelling a great myth. It is a theme that resonates through almost every recorded system of religious initiation from the past. No, the secrets of the Craft are not transplanted from a building site.

Sincere Masons can find themselves saying:

'I belong to an Order, which professes to confer Initiation upon the members who follow its lessons.'

'I have taken its Degrees. I am nominally a Master Mason, and even hold high rank in the Craft. In Masonry's theory and teaching I find much to admire and much that is spiritually stimulating. I also find much that I can dispense

with, and a great deal that seems inconsistent with the
Order's purpose and dignity.'

'I have learned certain truths from Masonry, and on the
whole I am a better person for being part of it. But I am
not an Initiate in any but the formal sense. Most of my
Brethren are in a similar plight, and, however eminent our
titular Masonic rank, we are as far from being Masters of
the Secret Science as any uninitiated person.'

'Our ritual says that Masonry is a high and serious subject.
It commits me to solemn personal vows, which I want to
take seriously. How can I realise the truths outlined in the
ritual, and become actually, not just in name, an Initiate and
a Master?'

These are questions that each new generation of Masons ask. And they
deserve answers. In this book I try to share my answers. You may find
these take unexpected forms and surprise you. If you are content to
remain only a nominal Initiate, if you do not seek a spiritual message,
my answers may mean little to you. If you prefer just to join in the social
side of our system, rather than struggle with its spiritual intentions,
then good luck to you. Enjoy the good company Masonry offers. But, if
you think the Craft is simply a way to gratify your ambition for personal
distinction, I ask you to consider this question. Do you really want to
be known as a shallow person who is only turned on by getting to
wear prettier and more elaborately embroidered aprons?

You may be thinking: 'Teach me. Show me the way, and I will
follow.' But you need to realise what you are embarking on. There are
many who start out eager, but, as the profounder things of Masonry
begin to be unveiled, they realise that each fresh disclosure of spiritual
values carries with it a new personal responsibility to live up to. I warn
you, it is better to remain in the dark than to have a vision of light and
then be unfaithful to it. And this larger knowledge of Masonry does not
come from casual reading of books or listening to lectures: it demands
long effort and persistent mental labour. It involves a revolution in

your previously cherished mental outlook and life-habits. The price of knowledge might be too high. You may decide you can walk no farther along this path; you may be discouraged; you may be unprepared for effort and sacrifice; you may drop back or choose to remain in the outer court of the initiate's temple. I do not intend to be unkind or critical, but this is a fact that I know to be true, and one which you will need to face. Many have been admitted to the Craft who are not yet ready, or do not even want real Initiation. The Mysteries of Freemasonry are a much bigger thing than most of us dream. They are greater than any outward organisation that tries to inculcate them. You can only internalise them when you are 'properly prepared'.

Masonry is not a secular society. It is a house of the spirit. It has to be lived in the spirit as well as in its ritual forms. We who live it know that this process continually tests us, like our ceremonies, which are dramatised images of life. If we do not pass the tests we remain self-inhibited from moving towards the larger knowledge and deeper experience that is only to be found at the veiled centre of Masonic allegory.

The purpose of Freemasonry is to help its members become Initiates in the Science of Life. If you want to know yourself, then Freemasonry offers a path to that knowledge. But beware; it is a spiritual adventure, only to be pursued by the athletic and adventurous mind.

Before you seek to explore the spiritual depths of the Craft, you should sit down and weigh the potential cost. Make sure that you are properly prepared to build upon a rock, not on an unstable personal foundation. As an Initiate, expect to suffer mental anguish. Progress in Masonic science involves great changes to yourself, your mental outlook and your ways of living. The prizes are immense, yet they are not for you alone. Initiation involves destroying your sense of personal self-hood to become a selfless instrument for the diffusion of light, wisdom and love to all beings.

If you follow this course; if you make your daily steps in Masonic knowledge; you may in time become a Living Stone in the Masonic Temple of perfected humanity.

# CHAPTER TWO

# WHAT IS INITIATION?

What do I mean when I talk of Initiation?

To become an Initiate, you need to know what is involved in the process and exactly what you are aspiring to become.

Let me explain by example.

Imagine you are a fish living in the dark depths of the sea. Your grasp of that way of life will be limited to what you can see and touch in your closed sub-aquatic world. You will know nothing of the land world, of the air world, of the sun and stars, of humans and their complex interests and civilisation. These will be things beyond the scope of your imagining. In Masonic terms, you would be hoodwinked and in a state of darkness.

If you were a fish of the calibre of Disney's Nemo and able to talk, you would probably be fiercely derisive about the existence of such a strange non-aqueous world, if it were suggested to you.

But if your level of perception could be changed, if you could be raised up to awareness and understanding of these things in the upper world, you would become a fishy initiate. You would know of ways of living, of secrets and mysteries of being, beyond the ken of your scaly compatriots. Your consciousness would be raised to a level that enables it to range far wider than theirs.

Whilst you are uninitiated you live in a state of constant darkness. You are only aware of your close surroundings. You accept as real only those things that you can see or touch, the things of the flesh. Everything of the spirit is uncertain, speculative or fanciful.

Your eyes are hoodwinked, and you fail to see the inner aspect of things. You do not behold the world of the spirit. Everything beyond the limitation of your physical senses is hidden. You may have notions, beliefs and strong convictions, and direct your life accordingly; but you lack direct contact with, and self-knowledge of, the spirit.

When you become an Initiate you learn certitude, contact and knowledge. There are degrees of advancement even among Initiates, but, whatever his (or her) degree, every Initiate has found and lives within her (or his) spiritual centre.

Non-initiates live from their gross senses. They live at their circumference, using reason, cognition and workaday intelligence. Initiates have a revolutionary inward experience that transforms their consciousness. It is one thing to be top of one's class, but quite another to be moved to a higher class altogether. As an Initiate you will move up a class in life-school. Masonically the Initiate is raised to a new order of consciousness.

You often hear myths about the Illuminati, but an Initiate is more than an Illuminate. Many good people and folk of genius are 'illuminated' as a result of their upward striving. Yet they stand only at the stage of progress denoted by the Second Degree. Symbolically, the dawn of their inward central Sun has not yet broken over their darkness; it has not yet heralded the aura of a hidden Great Light still to appear within them. An Initiate is not merely a good person, a sagacious person, a learned person or even a lovable person. You may be any or all of these, and still not be an Initiate.

An Initiate has taken the Third Degree. The Initiate's Sun is not just dawning as a glimmer of light on the mental horizon; it has risen to shine in their personal heaven. It is this mental state that confers the new dimension of consciousness. You are enabled to see more than the outside surfaces of things. You come to understand what is inside, and how it relates to all other things. As you become adept you learn to visualise the inner nature and moral condition of others, to read their minds and thoughts as easily as you read a newspaper. Distance, stone walls, or other interventions are no obstacle to your enhanced perception. You can refocus your consciousness in a way incomprehensible to the uninitiated.

What the average person sees as empty space, you see as a crowded world of life. Hidden threads form a living unity to link things and people that you once thought separate. You will be admitted to participation in the secrets and mysteries of life, made aware of the divine plan of the universe and of the place and purpose of humanity within it. You will perceive the sacred laws controlling its workings and identify with their fulfilment. With this insight come new faculties and wider powers, enabling you to do things you once thought impossible. Your new skills may appear miraculous and uncanny to others. But it is a fact of our Masonic Science that new consciousness gives rise to new faculties.

This change takes place within your spirit and consciousness, not in your outward appearance. And, though these changes might distinguish you from the popular world, that distinction should not make you feel superior. The way of the Initiate is the reverse of the way of the world. It must be accompanied by meekness, silence and a desire for self-effacement.

Great powers open up to you, and you may be tempted to use them for personal ends. But the true Initiate will refuse to misuse this insight. The only power you should desire personally is to avoid the lure of mortal fame and glory.

The life of the Initiate is hidden; it is not exposed to public scrutiny. It is an internal change in consciousness. If we think of great pivotal people who have worked for the spiritual and intellectual advancement of the race, we get an idea of the different order of consciousness that distinguishes them. Think of Isaac Newton, Marie Curie, Rosalind Franklin and Albert Einstein: each one had a mind that changed the human race. In such a way is the Initiate different from the dweller in darkness.

Initiation is a psychological change, an issue of personal consciousness and inward growth. You become an Initiate by spiritual effort – something that cannot be contrived. Rank comes as the result of interior development, not just taking part in ceremonies. Initiation is more than a ceremony, it is a process of learning, and ritual can only help to smooth the way to this knowledge.

Your learning may be as wide as Aristotle's or Bacon's, but that does not make you an Initiate. You may be unschooled in the world's wisdom and learning and yet still experience the supra-mental principle of transcendental knowledge that Masons call the Centre.

The purpose of all the ancient systems of Mysteries was to help individuals reach the Initiate state. This remains the Craft's purpose today. But that Initiation is not for your personal benefit. The aim of the Craft is not to make you complacent and self-satisfied. The Masonic path to attainment is too strenuous and painful for the majority to even wish to take. It involves the dying down and elimination of your sense of personal self-hood.

To attain a higher state you must lose your present way of life before you can gain a higher level.

Your motives for seeking Initiation must be altruistic. As an Initiate you will not become enlightened until you become selfless and impersonal; you must dispel your own darkness. The uninitiated are blind to the limitation set by their own egos. Since the blind lead the blind only into ditches, Initiates – individuals of vision and who know the Plan of life – are needed for the world's guidance and salvation.

Darwin tells us that in Nature we find four kingdoms of consciousness, three prehuman and one human. It is unthinkable that evolution should stop and come to a cul-de-sac in the human, so we can visualise a fifth kingdom. This is a kingdom of Initiates. At present we are animals with divine possibilities, and the savage legacy of our primeval origins must be driven below the threshold of our consciousness before those possibilities can come into play.

It is this fifth kingdom – the kingdom of the Initiates – that Masonry invites us first to contemplate and then to enter. That is why five upward steps lead from the First to the Second Degree. That is why we are told to lift our eyes to a bright five-pointed star whose rising brings peace and salvation to the faithful and obedient. So, too, we develop Five Points of Fellowship and self-identification, and the number five recurs so prominently in our system.

Nature loves the number five. Look at the hosts of five-petalled flowers and five-pointed leaves she produces. Our human senses are five, and our hands and feet split to form five extremities each. They are part of Nature's efforts to prepare her creatures for eventual advancement to a kingdom that, in our Secret Masonic Science, is always associated with the number five.

The geometrical symbolist will think of the five kingdoms in terms of the point, the line, the square, the cube, and finally the pentagon or five-pointed star. The physiologist thinks in terms of the cell and its compound structures. The psychologist, taking x as the simplest conscious mode (the mineral), will equate the plant with

$x^2$, the animal with $x^3$, man with $x^4$, and the Initiate with $x^5$: each new kingdom involving an extra dimension of consciousness.

But every kingdom is self-contained. It is shut off, as though by closed bulkheads, and no leap from a lower to a higher kingdom is possible save on one condition – a previous death to the kingdom below.

No biologist can trace the point when decaying clay gave way to minute lichen. Nor can the point where vegetable food becomes animal tissue be isolated. And at what stage of evolution did sensory tissue permit the miraculous birth of human intelligence? These transitions are not always physically demonstrable, but they occur on subtle levels, in the gaps between the rungs of our symbolic ladder. All we know is that change occurs, and the death of something precedes every new and higher begetting.

When you aspire to pass from the merely human to become a Masonic Initiate, it will involve a symbolic death. This is what our Third Degree teaches us. Such a death was always the culminating feature of the Ancient Mysteries, and it remains so with us. When our ritual says that Masonry finally teaches you how to die, something deep is involved. This phrase shows that the Craft prescribes not only a special technique of living but also a definite technique of dying. This is our Secret Science of mystical death and resurrection. It is the Secret Science of Initiation, which a properly prepared candidate comes to learn.

The Egyptian Book of the Dead is an old example of this science. Buddhism also employs similar rituals. Other sublime examples are in use in our country today, but this is a delicate and deeply concealed subject, never openly discussed. It may only be learned from the private instruction of the Master to whom the Candidate is affiliated.

For the benefit of the spiritually aware, our ritual hints at this deeper teaching. The unenlightened person dreads death in any form and wishes to hear as little about it as possible. But a mystical dying, of the kind which brings about the making of a Master Mason, results in raising you to the fifth kingdom. It makes you an Initiate. You 'suffer a sea-change into something rich and strange'.

But this change is subjective, occurring in the deep parts of your soul and transforming your consciousness by renewing your mind. Other people will see no difference in your outward appearance. You will return to the companions of your former toils and resume your usual activities. Yet your whole being has been raised to a higher power and is reinforced by an inner life of a higher quality.

In Masonry, this is called being made perfect. At this stage you have fulfilled your part in Nature's fourth kingdom and are properly prepared to enter the fifth. In real Initiation a solemn psychological crisis tears apart your mental veil. You hear your inner defences ripping and crashing, then a trumpet blast banishes the silence of your mind. The delicate nerve webbing that had shut off your perception of super-sensual things is torn from your eyes, and a blinding blaze of light makes you an Initiate.

You may feel that here I seem to be moving beyond Masonry into the realm of religion. But I am not. I am bridging and unifying them. Both deal with the same subject, and both have spiritual goals, but their approaches are different.

What is the difference between a Masonic Initiate and a religious one? To Initiates it is given to understand, via the hidden mysteries of nature and science, the mystery of the centre. To the uninitiated all these things are veiled in allegory. The religious Initiate takes these things as matters of blind faith and book teaching, and so fails to experience the force of their Truth. The Masonic Initiate learns spiritual knowledge as a practical living science, and experiences an exact understanding of truths of which the non-initiate has but shadowy notions.

As a Master Mason, during the rituals and the meeting of the Lodge, you will live the experience of initiation and the expansion of consciousness that this involves.

# CHAPTER THREE

# THE FIRST MASONIC STEP TO INITIATION

In the early stages of your initiation, Masonry teaches you two key lessons:

'Know yourself.'

'You are a microcosm of the universe.'

You are taught to know yourself, since to understand yourself teaches you about the cosmos and the sacred law that runs it. To know yourself you must think about everything that lives and moves.

You are taught that you are a microcosm, because the process that creates every human being takes a single cell and develops it into a living, conscious entity. This is a symbolic copy of the evolution of the entire universe. As a child you know only that which is finite and limited, but within your mind is the potential to become aware of the infinite and illimitable. A single acorn contains a potential forest of oaks.

## THE FIRST-DEGREE TRACING BOARD

To help the Apprentice understand these truths, Freemasonry offers the First-Degree Tracing Board (see Plate 1). This set of symbols is to focus your thoughts and guide your meditation. At first sight it seems to be a casual collection of the emblems found in every Masonic Lodge. But, as your Masonic insight develops, order and purpose emerge from it. You begin to see it is a diagram of the material, mental and spiritual elements in us all. These are shown as the Earth, the Intermediate Firmament and the Heavens

The floor represents your physical state, or body: your lower or material nature. The sky, with its Sun, Moon and stars, stands for your mind or intellectual nature. But the blazing star, or Glory, in the centre represents your ultimate spiritual core. This Bright Morning Star dominates the centre of the diagram and lights the whole board with its blinding rays.

Masonic ritual explains these ancient symbols of a human being.

## *The Earth*

The Earth represents your physical nature. It is that part of yourself where your natural consciousness is normally focused. This lowest element in us is shown as a chequer-work floor made up of black and white squares of equal size. This shows that everything in the material world is split into two opposite aspects. Even our limbs, organs and brains are duplicated.

You can think of nothing terrestrial without being compelled to recognise the existence of its complementary opposite. Light and darkness; good and evil; right and left; birth and death; adversity and prosperity; male and female; pleasure and pain. These are the dualisms inherent in the physical world of which we are a part.

Experience of these opposites is essential to human growth. Our existence consists of perpetual movement, like chessmen, from a white square to a black and from a black to a white. These moves continually test us and form our character; we grow as the result of our responses to both good and bad conditions. For how can we say that one class of experience is better or worse than the other? Each is necessary and each complementary.

New brethren sometimes ask, 'Is it not our duty to keep to the white squares and avoid the black?' The answer is No. It is quite beyond your power to do so, for every good has the seed of evil in it, and every evil contains germs of good. This does not mean that you must prefer evil to good, darkness to light, or court adversity for its own sake. It merely means that the joys and sorrows, the lights and shades of mundane existence must be accepted with equal thanks.

When evil or sorrowful conditions dominate, they should be recognised as having the same educational value as their opposites. Naturally we prefer pleasant conditions, but the sacred law governing life pays no heed to our personal desires. It is a hard teacher that leads us from temporal to eternal values. We find its silent thrust moving us on from one coloured square to another despite our will, and often before we are aware of change.

As the seasons wheel and turn, so health overripens into decay and death. This, in turn, engenders a spring of new life. Prosperity that seemed unending can wither away, and poverty can rise to sudden wealth.

As you read this book you are awake, but the mere act of living will soon force you to sleep. You have been born into this world and, as a consequence, you are under a sentence of death. There is no hill without its dale, no sweet without its corresponding bitter, no light of day without its dark of night.

It is the same with our standards of conduct, our ethics. We label our actions good or bad, but the distinction is an arbitrary convention. The ideal of one age becomes a fault in the next. A well-motivated generous act can produce consequences disastrous to the person it is meant to benefit. An evil act may create unexpected good. A personal virtue pushed to extremes hardens into a vice, whilst a fool who pursues his folly far enough may learn wisdom.

Our distinctions of good and bad, true and false, are nothing more than the personal or collective view of our society at that moment. To the clearer sight of the Initiate things are neither one nor the other, they are just facts of life needing no qualifying. As Shakespeare put it: 'The web of our life is a mingled yarn, good and ill together.'

The first task of a Candidate for Wisdom is to learn to rise above material dualism. You must adjust your outlook to see beyond the material. You must become master of your lower nature and bodily tendencies. You must learn to stand mentally detached from the inevitable fluctuations of fortune and emotion that afflict you and to regard the ups and downs, the whites and blacks, of life as of equal formative value to you.

Our Ritual says: the square pavement is for the high priest to walk upon. This means you are to think of yourself as high priest of the temple of your body, and as such you must walk upon the ever-changing events of existence, whilst standing above them. You must learn to remain stable, serene and detached amid circumstances that elate or deject those whose emotions are focused upon the transient and unreal.

You must not try to pick out a timorous and pleasant way by walking only on the white squares. With confidence and strength of mind you must also cross the black ones. Learn to perceive good and evil, pleasure and pain, birth and death, adversity and prosperity – and all the other opposites signified by the squares – as alternating aspects of a single process. Welcome each one for the role it can play in your growth.

The square pavement is surrounded by skirtwork. This implies that the sacred law encircles and permeates existence, binding all the chequer-work into unity.

To the Grand Geometrician of the Universe darkness and light are both alike and both good. So must you learn to recognise the equal worth of the blacks and whites of temporal existence. Whatever your lot at a given moment, whether darkness or light be your portion, around you is the skirtwork, the trust in the sacred law, and neither in ups or downs nor in life or death can you evade it or stray beyond its reach.

However chequered your experience, however far you travel among the lights and shades of existence, you can never fall off the map. As the board signifies, in whichever direction you move – North, South, East or West – your road must eventually bring you to the surrounding unity. There all opposites are resolved, and all dualism is transcended. By this chequered floor and indented skirtwork the board shows that the Plan of the Great Architect is the warp and weft of all existence. The rule of the sacred law encloses and impinges upon all points of our being.

An implicit cable runs round the skirtwork, emerging as visible tassels at the four corners. This signifies the current of hidden energy circulating through the Universe and split into four modes. The Ancients called these modes the four primal elements of Fire, Air, Water and Earth. These energies in their infinite permutations and combinations compose the bedrock of the universe.

### *The Firmament, or Heavens*

The First-Degree Tracing Board shows the Firmament above the Earth. To put it more romantically, above the material earthiness of your body, soars the heaven of your mind. The symbol of the firmament stands for the complex, psychological structure of your consciousness.

The heavens are shown as an in-between area screening our world from the celestial worlds beyond. You also are a microcosm. Your mind and ego form a similar mental firmament that sits between your temporal physical nature and your ultimate self.

The Firmament stands for your psychological make-up, and the Tracing Board shows it as the Heavens, just as it showed your physical body as the Earth. This Firmament can be divided into three parts:

1. Your emotional nature, which is shown in the Tracing Board by a group of seven stars (planets) in the South-East corner.

2. Your natural instincts or lower carnal mind, which you have in common with creatures with less complex brains. This is the instinctive, reptilian part of your brain that decides which of the famous four Fs you will use to respond to anything you meet.* This is also in the South-East corner, where it is symbolised by the Moon – which is surrounded by the stars, showing that the mind and emotions work in conjunction.

3. Your higher mind and controlling will. This is the self-conscious intellect that makes you a moral being. It is symbolised by the Sun, in the North-East corner of the Tracing Board.

This symbolism draws on ancient ideas about the mind that said that a Sun, Moon and stars exist within the person of each of us, as well as in the outward sky. In one sense the external sun, moon and stars are truly present in us, since their radiation is continually beating down upon us, penetrating our bodies, and building subtle influences into us. Without their existence no life would be possible on our planet. But the symbolism carries a deeper message than

* *Fight it, Feed on it, Flee from it, or Reproduce with it. (NB. The F in Reproduce is silent.)*

this. In addition to your physical husk, you possess other symbolic interior bodies. Each is a distinct capsule of mental responses, and they all serve as the vehicles of your emotions and instincts.

Freemasonry teaches that you are a composite being – hardly surprising if you are to think of yourself as a microcosm of the living universe. Your spirit can learn to wear not one but many bodies, each having its appropriate function and sphere of action.

Your senses, emotions and mental processes are normally blended together. They can, however, be separated by careful study and reflection. In a similar way your inner symbolic bodies are largely intertwined, but they also can be separated by mental study.

Your physical husk is the densest and most external of them all. You can think of it as the overcoat or rough shell that acts as a container for the others. As it is the outermost and coarsest, it is the first to decay and decompose into its elements, leaving your mind, after its death, standing clothed in more ethereal sheaths.

Everyday experience shows you that there are emotions going on within you that are quite detached from your conscious will. Passions, worthy or ignoble, surge through you without obvious cause. The phenomena of dream states, sleep-walking and remote viewing suggest that we might possess powers of action and motion that act outside our physical machine.

Your emotions, your desires, their alternating forms of attraction and repulsion, have a life of their own. They continue their activity in ways that your conscious mind may only occasionally be aware of. This emotional life can be thought of as having a body of its own. This is the starry or astral body, drawn in the Tracing Board as the seven wandering stars (which are really planets). These astral lights are wanderers, moving around the Sun that controls and holds them in check whilst seeming to dance attendance on the Moon. They symbolise the range of our emotional urges, which are also restless wanderers. They are never still, and are apt to break away from their true courses unless held in check by their governing centre, the will.

We know that our mental faculties function quite independently of either our senses or our emotions. How often have you gone to sleep thinking about a problem, only to wake the following morning with the answer clear in your mind? The subconscious mind acts while the body sleeps; it works out problems that we cannot solve when we are awake. Being a field to itself, with an independent life of its own, it can also be regarded as having a body – the mental or lunar body, symbolised by the Moon. For, just as the moon is a satellite moving with and illumining the earth, so in us the reasoning mind is a satellite moving with and enlightening the body, but it has no light of its own and shines only by reflection from the superior solar luminary.

Freemasonry uses the symbols of the Moon and stars to represent our mental and emotional natures. These are our bodies terrestrial, and they serve a useful purpose in our temporal life. We use them to govern the night – the night, in this Masonic instance, meaning our rational minds. This rational self is inevitably blind to spiritual things until assisted by the light from the Centre.

This light from the centre is the Sun, shown in the North-East corner of the Board. This concept is even more difficult to explain, for this Sun is outside the physical and mental order of things that we have experience of, although Freemasonry says it is present in each of us. It is the mainspring and driving power of our personal system, as the natural sun is the central control of the solar system.

This Masonic Sun is vaster than our planet, and is self-radiant, while our Earth is dense and non-luminous. So our metaphysical Sun is far grander and wiser than the elementary personality revolving round it. It presides over this persona and rules the day, from the perpetual light of our spiritual world.

The Masonic Sun is our Higher Self. It is a large spiritual area in each of us not subject to time and space. It lives in daylight and freedom beyond the dark prison-house of the mundane personality, over which, never sleeping, it hovers and watches.

If you become spiritually awake you realise that your external personality, the face you put on for the world, is only a fragment of your true self. You are more than what is contained between your hat and your boots; the mundane side of yourself shows the outer world only a limited part of your individuality. You are like an iceberg, with the major part of yourself, beyond your brain-consciousness, hidden upon a higher mental plane.

Your inner symbolic Sun is the spirit, the incorruptible principle that makes you human. It is your body celestial. Your lesser vehicles of flesh, emotion and mind are bodies terrestrial, inherently mutable and corruptible. They wax, age and decay like the garments they are. They change with your changing personalities, but your spiritual Centre remains constant. It does not fail as your body ages.

Platonist and other mystical schools call this solar symbol the *Augoeides*, the self-radiant body; it is always drawn as the Sun. It is well known in Egyptian hieroglyphs, appearing as the figure of Ra carried upon a boat, and is referred to in our ritual as the Sun shining in his strength.

The Masonic Sun symbol is placed in the North-East corner of the Tracing Board. And it was in the North-East corner of the Lodge that your physical person was placed when you were newly made a Mason. There you were placed as a foundation stone. There you were directed to build a perfect structure. Your spirit is that superstructure. With time and effort you build this super-physical structure from your personality in the physical world. This spirit is both fulcrum and foundation.

Whatever we do, or think, with our physical body effects changes to our spirit. We can strengthen or weaken it, clarify or cloud it. Freemasonry teaches us that we should work towards a state where all our thoughts, words and actions may ascend pure and unpolluted into our spirit. The spirit is the enduring vessel where our purest activities are gathered up and preserved.

Your present character, your dominant tendencies are the net product of everything you have done and thought. You are today what you have made yourself by your past actions. Your future destiny is moulded by your present conduct and thoughts. We are all, at every moment, silently building our inner spirit.

Freemasonry likens this work to the job of erecting King Solomon's Temple. The various building materials are prepared at a distance. They are taken to Jerusalem and put together silently, without sound of axe or hammer. The aim is to build a perfect structure, of which every part is properly prepared and ready to fit in with the rest. All this is metaphor, picture language, describing the work of spirit-building that every Mason engages in.

King Solomon's Temple is a metaphor for the human spirit. It is the superstructure every Mason is engaged in raising. We are building a temple not made with hands or subject to decay. Our every thought, word and deed contributes new material for our invisible construction.

For good or ill all our actions are assembled and silently shaped into our spirit. We must strive to ensure we contribute stones and timber of a quality and finish worthy of the Great Architect's design.

### The Blazing Star, or Glory, in the Centre

You have seen how the Tracing Board showed the Earth and Heavens as your physical and mental faculties. But it also shows another element, the spiritual essence that is the ultimate root of your being. It is this part of you which affiliates with the Great Architect of the Sacred Law. This ultimate spirit is difficult to express in words. It is beyond the grasp of the reasoning mind, and it has no form. Perceiving this spirit is the great goal of the Initiate.

In the First-Degree Tracing Board the presence of this spirit is only suggested. It is symbolised as a Blazing Star in the East. Its bright rays flood the picture and far outshine the light of the Sun, Moon and stars. These are only subordinate luminaries, instruments through which this supreme light from the centre is mediated.

Being the very root and core of our being, the Spirit is called by us Masons, the Centre. When we come to find and use it, it is the point from which no Mason can ever err.

In the Platonist and Hermetic systems this Centre was called the One, or the Good. It is the unity into which our complex, scattered faculties can be collected and summed up. It is also known as the Monad, or sometimes the Paternal Monad. It is the primal and parent source of our temporal personality which projects into the world of space and form.

It is this Centre, this supreme spiritual essence in us, which is Masonically described as our vital and immortal principle. It is the supreme light of all. Like the Master's light in the East, it never goes out, even though all other lights fail. It is the light that alone illumines the darkness of our Third Degree. But even there it is perceived at first as but a mere glimmer. For those who learn to perceive it, this Morning Star will break forth in full splendour, its rising bringing peace and salvation to those who faithfully and obediently pursue it.

The goal of all mystical attainment, whether in Masonry or elsewhere, is the union of the human with the divine consciousness. This is why the First-Degree Tracing Board puts the Blazing Star at its centre and makes it the most conspicuous feature of the diagram. It symbolises the divine principle in yourself that you must seek to make one with the root of your being.

## PRACTICAL WORK FOR THE INITIATE

So far I've only discussed the symbolic philosophy of the First Tracing Board. I have shown how it reveals the secrets of your constitution and the more hidden paths of your nature. But it goes on to indicate how you should put this theoretical science into practical use. Only those who perform the internal work come to know the profound truth of this Masonic doctrine. The information remains useless theory unless you reduce it to practice and learn it by living it.

But where do you find this practical instruction manual? It is there in the Tracing Board. To understand it you need to look at the other emblems in the diagram. These are:

1. Some working tools and models casually spread about the floor. The meaning of these is obvious and is explained in the ordinary Lodge teaching, so I do not need to enlarge upon it here.

2. An emblem consisting of a point within a circle bounded by two parallel lines.

3. An altar, on which rest the three main emblematic Lights of Masonry (the Square, the Compasses and the open Volume of the Sacred Law). From this altar a ladder of innumerable steps leads to the Firmament and thence to infinity.

4. Three pillars, referred to in the ritual as Doric, Ionic, and Corinthian. Their pedestals are on the Earth and their capitals in the Heavens.

## *The Point within a Circle*

This geometrical emblem conveys intangible and spiritual truths. Its meaning does not start to become clear until after the Second Degree, and its full meaning and practical value is only fully revealed in the Plan, or Tracing Board of the Centre. However, even at this stage of advancement it is a useful symbol for you to meditate on. I offer this description to aid and direct your meditation:

> The circle is that of infinity whose centre is everywhere and circumference nowhere. It is Infinity shrunk and compressed to a point, but a point from which it is possible to consciously expand to Infinite Being. Your personal temporal self is but a separated individualised point in the ocean of the universal spirit encompassing you, but, by renouncing and dying to the sense of your personal self, you will transcend it and, losing the sense of separateness, grow into conscious union with the one indivisible life which comprehends all.

> The parallel lines bounding the circle tell you that this one indivisible life is everywhere characterised by two opposite aspects bound together in perpetual equilibrium. Spirit and Matter, the Formless and the Formal, Freedom and Necessity, inflexible Justice and boundless Mercy – these are parallels permeating the universe on all its planes, present in every atom and cell.

> They are held together in eternal balance at one neutral central point where these opposites blend into unity. That point in yourself is the Centre, to find which you must follow a middle way, a straight and narrow path, turning neither to the right hand nor the left, and in every pursuit having the eternal unity in view.

## *The Altar*

The altar is a double cube, worked from a rough ashlar into perfect six-sided form. This is a symbol of how your mind will be when made perfect in all its parts. The concealed underside resting on the Earth stands for the hidden, submerged depths of your subconscious. The four sides facing the four quarters of the Lodge signify your human elementary nature brought into a balance as a harmonious, foursquare foundation stone for a spiritual building.

The upper side is exposed to the light of the Bright Morning Star. On its surface rest the three Great Lights of Masonry. This is the reverse of the concealed underside and represents the consciousness of a purified personality turning away from mundane interests and facing towards the source of light.

When King Solomon completed his temple he dedicated it to the Most High. By doing this he invoked into it a divine presence that appeared as a Great Light. This is known as the descent of the Shekinah. The glory of this Bright Morning Star flooded the whole building, showing what is possible in the person of every dedicated Mason.

This is the great goal of Initiation. You must be an altar made from earth, the builder of it, the offering upon it, the priest who serves it; then you must ascend the great spiritual ladder to achieve union with the Centre beyond the Heavens.

This upward ascent of the human mind and spirit has been described in the literature of all ages. It is spoken of as the Ladder of Perfection, the journey of the mind into The Most High, the ascent of the mystical mountain, the Way, and the Path. These are all terms for the same truth and the same process.

The steps of that ladder are innumerable, for the heights are reached not by a single bound or sudden translation, but by persistent effort. Every act and thought of daily life must be concentrated upon the goal. Even while sleeping, the devoted Mason will dream of climbing the steps of this ladder to the Infinite.

These symbols are to remind us that we are beings striving to climb out of the mud of the unconscious. We are moving towards the perfection of our spiritual being. The altar symbolises our struggle to organise our human form to a stage where it is possible for us to look ahead to our eventual destiny and to utilise the sacred law to realise it.

Our daily step in Masonic wisdom comes as we strive to raise our consciousness from the level of the material to that of the spiritual. We are trying to knit our minds with the universal spirit that is the Cosmos. This is what is signified by the six-sided altar, and the symbolic ladder of ascent that stretches from it into the limitless light.

Long before you reach full union with the Centre you will become aware of stirrings of subtle relations with it. This unitive process is gradual, for if it was abrupt it would blind rather than enlighten. If it comes before you are properly prepared, it can confound and wither, rather than heal and sustain. Hence the need within our system for the candidate to be properly prepared in each Degree. When the high light of the Centre has dawned on unprepared candidates in its full splendour and majesty, they have found themselves unable to bear it. They have begged that it might be removed from them till they are better able to endure its rays.

### The Three Pillars

Long before you are ready for direct perception of the Centre, convincing internal evidence will grow in your mind to show your growing union with it. How will you become aware of this? By the dawning within yourself of that light's three primary attributes. The Sun's white light is invisible till passed through a prism that decomposes it into seven constituent colours, of which three are primaries. When the spiritual light of the centre falls upon the prism of the human spirit, its sevenfold properties begin to manifest, and of these there are three primaries. Masonry calls them *Wisdom*, *Strength* and *Beauty*.

They are symbolised in the Tracing Board by three Pillars that spring from the ground. They rise into the heavens, yet support no visible structure. The spiritual powers they represent are prominent features in the spirit of an Initiated Master Mason.

To ordinary ears *Wisdom*, *Strength*, *Beauty*, are nothing but sentimental abstracts. But in Masonic science they are concrete realities. They constitute the very substance of our spirits.

To understand what wisdom means to the Initiate, you must turn to those chapters of the Book of Wisdom, where our Grand Master Solomon describes it and relates its influence upon himself. He describes the conditions upon which it may be attained. You must learn that the true beginning of *Wisdom* is the desire for mental discipline, and that to acquire *Wisdom* you must develop your intellect – but that is a matter to be addressed more fully in the Second Degree.

To understand *Strength* you must first be content to still your finite natural energies. Only then will you learn what is referred to in the Sacred Law as the power of the highest. In stillness you will feel its tide surge through your being, enabling you to achieve beneficent work that normally you would not be capable of.

Every Initiate taps into the secret hidden sources of power that endow you with extended faculties and abnormal capacity for work. However, at the same time you must learn the conditions under which that power may be exercised. For, if it is put to selfish personal ends, its secrets will not be a blessing but a curse. Its misuse is fraught with moral and spiritual peril.

*Beauty* is even harder to express in words. It is the ultimate form into which the life-essences of a creature crystallise. A flower, for instance, is the beauty or glory of a plant. It is the expression in which the essences of the plant culminate. It displays beauty as geometrical form, colour and fragrance. Similarly in humans, as the spirit labours towards perfection it takes on a structural beauty, It crystallises into a geometrical form expressive of its qualities. It changes from a shapeless dull mass to become self-radiant, and shine as the stars. Any one star (or spirit) differs from another in its glory, just as one flower differs in shape and colour from another. But each expresses an aspect of the glory of the Centre.

These changes to the spirit cannot be seen with your physical eyes. But Initiates, whose inner vision is open to the spiritual world, can confirm the awesome beauty of spirits that have been shaped by the laws of divine geometry. They speak of perceiving perfection in form and radiance.

Our three Pillars represent a trinity of attributes that are born within every Candidate upon whose inner altar celestial light descends. Like the Master and Wardens of the Lodge who always act in concert, so *Wisdom*, *Strength* and *Beauty* are inseparable. They are a triple cord, not easily broken. They are three that agree as one and bear witness within us to the reality of the Centre.

If *Wisdom* from on high visits you, *Strength* comes with it. *Beauty* shapes the spirit's structure into true form and irradiates it with spiritual graces.

### *Entering the Temple*

At the Temple at Jerusalem there was a gate called Beautiful. It was at that gate that Initiates of Wisdom wrought works of Power. Their feats amazed the unenlightened crowd that filled Solomon's porch. In the same way the uninitiated of today stand amazed at the possibilities that open before advanced spirits.

When you submit yourself to our Masonic rites you profess to enter them in the name of your Supreme Being. You admit that to seek the Light is the predominant wish of your heart. By that act the light of the Centre is solemnly invoked upon you, and you forge a spiritual link with it.

As an Apprentice you enter our Order in its temporal and visible aspect. But you also become spiritually joined with the Great Architect and the Sacred Law. You sign on as a worker in the spiritual building scheme of humanity and accept the work of a Freemason. A subtle change is wrought in your spirit that makes you different from those who have not been Initiated.

It matters not whether you, or those who perform our rites for your benefit, are aware of this truth. Indeed you may be long in awaking to it, but be assured that our rituals, even if performed with imperfect knowledge of their value, are never worked in vain. They are spiritually trenchant rites. When a ray of that light from the Centre, whose rainbow-like elements are *Wisdom*, *Strength* and *Beauty*, falls upon your spirit, it stays with you whether you profit by it or choose to neglect it.

You must learn how the Tracing Boards disclose the secrets of your own nature and declare the practical work you must undertake. If you do this, then you will realise the intentions you adopted on entering the Craft. Nothing has been revealed here but that which has been tested and found true by the experience of Brethren who have faithfully followed the path traced for them in our various Degree Boards.

You will have to test and learn these truths for yourself. Books, lectures and explanations may help, but they can never be more than secondary. This makes them unsatisfying evidence of things that can only be proved by personal experience. You can never be book-taught or lecture-fed into knowledge of the Mysteries of the Craft. For, as the Tracing Board shows, Masonry is a way, a truth, and a life.

To learn that way you must walk it and take its steps yourself. To know that truth, you must personally labour for it and become it. To share that life you must live it so that it lives in you.

The path from West to East is not easy to tread. The altar of sacrifice and obliteration of oneself is not kindled to a clear flame without invoking a searing pain. The stairway to the heights is steep. It calls on you for fortitude and prudence, for personal righteousness and steadfast purpose.

But all that you surrender is replaced with compensating help and blessings. As you mount the great ladder, the pains of the way change to joys, as broad vistas of understanding open out before you. Wisdom descends upon you as a sanctifying and increasing light. You become strengthened by a mightier Power than your own. From your once hoodwinked eyes the veils fall, and through the gate Beautiful you will be able to look forth into the land of far distances.

May these things become true for all whom these words reach.

# CHAPTER FOUR

# THE SECOND MASONIC STEP TO INITIATION

If you want to move forwards through the Degrees of the Craft you must work to convert the lessons of each Degree into living progress. In the First Degree you pledged yourself to persevere steadfastly through the formal rites. To make the teaching of this Second Degree live in you, you must now persevere in the important job of converting those rites into reality.

If you fail to work on the task of understanding and controlling your physical body, you will be an Initiate in name only. Without meditative work to subdue the impulses of your body, your spirit will be unable to find the path to the Centre. Our ceremonies will remain ritual formalities without value; they will be husks whose kernel lies unseen in the darkness.

Often the three Degrees are taken rapidly, sometimes in three successive months. It is unlikely that in so brief a time you will grasp their implications in full. You will have been furnished with a system of instruction in spiritual advancement, but the first step of Initiation – understanding and controlling your emotions and instincts – will have been too rapid for you to fully grasp it. To develop, you are expected to focus your future life on establishing and maintaining this awareness and control. But it may take you years of thought and effort to work out how to do so.

Our rituals may not open your mind at the moment they are given. You may not immediately see the light and deeper perception of Truth that Initiation offers; often further spiritual work will be needed before you attain the higher orders of consciousness. But sudden awakening *can* happen, if you come properly prepared in heart and intention. Some derive a truly magical stimulus, a permanent quickening of their spirit's dormant or repressed faculties during the rite. (This desirable result will occur more often if everyone involved in the ritual fully understands exactly what he, or she, is doing in terms of the emotional experience the Candidate undergoes and the process of teaching the steps of the Craft that the rituals are meant to impart. If the Initiating Officers understand the process of the Craft and work closely together to realise it as well as they can, they will make the experience more meaningful for the Candidate.)

Usually the quickening of consciousness reveals itself slowly and gradually. It comes as the result of reflection upon the Craft's doctrine and symbolism, and from attempts to follow the path of life mapped out by its teaching. The Tracing Boards are there to stimulate your imagination and help you to reflect.

Before starting work in the Second Degree you must learn in full the lessons of the First Tracing Board. They should be more than theoretical ideas: you should be living them out in personal experience. When you have reached this stage, you are ready to extend your researches into the more hidden paths of your nature and the science of yourself. But beware; the spiritual work of the Second Degree must not be entered upon lightly. It can lead to deep water and situations of real mental danger. It should only be undertaken when you are morally, mentally and emotionally prepared.

Before passing to the Second Degree, you must complete your labours on the groundwork of your personality. The ground you clear must be both purified and adorned with virtue. Your spirit must become worthy to be offered at the temple of the Most High. When it is ready, as was the case with Solomon's House, the Shekinah will descend upon it and fill it with light and glory.

## THE SECOND-DEGREE TRACING BOARD

The Second-Degree Tracing Board (see Plate 2) portrays a landscape of open country, through which runs a river, flowing over a weir and making a waterfall; beside the water grows a single ear of corn. All this is placed on the South side of the Board, and from this sunny region a man approaches a Porchway, protected by an armed guard, which gives access to a spiral stairway. At the top of the stair is a second guard and an upper concealed chamber beyond. The ritual tells us that the approaching man (the Candidate) will visualise the words 'Holiness to the Lord' blazing above him.

The purpose of this Board is personal. If you want to work the Second Degree you must allow it to speak to your intellect. This Degree is about the higher, mental reaches of your nature.

The First Degree taught you to lay the foundation of a new life in the sacred law. You were told to erect a temple purged of the weaknesses of the flesh upon the ground floor of your natural personality. Now, with your animal instinct beautified with virtue and adorned by grace of character, you are bidden to move upwards, to gain instruction and experience a higher level of your being.

Body, mind, spirit – these are the three storeys of our building, the three degrees of our being, and each has its own secrets and mysteries.

We considered the mysteries of the ground floor, the body, in the First Degree. But these are as nothing compared with those of the mind, which we study in the Second Degree. The mysteries of your mind are hidden in the middle chamber, which you symbolically entered during the ceremony. And, if you come properly prepared, you can ascend to this chamber and delight in its provisions. But this is only another step on the way; higher still, above the middle chamber of the mind, lies the supreme mystery of the spirit, which awaits you when you are raised to the Third Degree. This is the Sanctum Sanctorum, the most holy place, and can be entered only by those who become the high priests of their spirit.

### *The River and the Fall of Water*

The man who has crossed the river and is approaching from the sunlight of the South represents you. He typifies an aspirant who is enlightened enough to break away from the bondage of the senses and seek life upon higher levels.

Crossing the flowing water of the river symbolises a clean break with your old life and the cleansing of yourself ready for a new one. The South indicates mental enlightenment, and is in contrast with the mental darkness of the North. In the First Degree you were placed in the North-East (the sunrise line of the day of most light); then, to show that you were now mentally prepared to face darkness in your mental condition, you were placed in the South-East (the sunrise line of the day of most dark) for the Second Degree.

## *The Ear of Corn*

The ear of corn growing by the water is a key symbol. Our body is the Earth, given to each of us to plant in it a worthy spirit. Corn is an emblem of seed, or the principle of immortality, growing in the soil of our mortal bodies.

The spiritual principle within us springs out of our personal Earth. Its growth is gradual, corresponding with our three Degrees: first the blade, then the ear, after that the full corn in the ear. As the growth progresses, the latent faculties of the spirit unfold from an embryonic state into maturity, perfection and power.

What better counsel is there to offer you than to tell you of the infinite degrees of consciousness available to you if you faithfully follow the path now opening before you? Learn that the ear of corn is the omniscient principle already planted within you, waiting only to be nourished by your own efforts to grow and bear fruit in plenty. Just as modern physicists have discovered that, locked up within the atom, are energies of amazing power waiting to be liberated and harnessed to use, so also, locked up within you, are concentrated, unimaginable riches just awaiting liberation.

## *The Porchway*

The man who has crossed the river is hastening towards a Porchway.

This porch is said to be that of Solomon's Temple. But, symbolically, that temple had more than one Porchway. Masonic lore says it had three main entrances, each representing one of the ways to approach the Truth of the Centre.

1. You can seek Truth through The Gate Beautiful. To do this you must show long-term allegiance to spiritual beauty and learn to practice emotional and aesthetic awareness.

2. You may choose to enter through The Gate of Works. This path involves altruistic service, selfless activity and sacrifice for the general good of humankind.

3. The third way to Truth is an intellectual path, through The Gate of Wisdom. This perception of Truth arises from enlightened mental application.

All three gates lead to the Centre, but The Gate of Wisdom (or Knowledge), is known to Masons as Solomon's Porch, because it was the gate used by King Solomon himself and is the focus of the work of a Fellowcraft.

The Second Degree is concerned with the development of the intellect. As a Fellowcraft you are urged extend your researches to encompass the hidden mysteries of nature and science. Thereby you gain first knowledge and then wisdom. To pass through Solomon's Porch you must devote your mind to philosophy and the study of cosmic law, in all its moral, intellectual and physical aspects. You must discipline your mind to see beyond the façade and to perceive the reality within. You must learn to ascend gently and gradually, as by a spiral path, to plane above plane of widening consciousness and understanding.

Philosophy is the Porchway to Truth, and its pursuit widens human understanding. As a Fellowcraft you are told to devote yourself to such of the liberal arts and sciences as lie within the compass of your attainments. The pursuit of abstract truth frees your mind, detaching it from surface interests and eliminating prejudices. This mental quest teaches you to discriminate between the illusory and the real and prepares you for the perception of super-physical truths.

Our Second-Degree ritual is less spectacular than those of the other Degrees, because the type of mental work it symbolises cannot readily be dramatised. This Degree assists your psychological development, and you must labour privately to discover the best way for you to advance. Sources of inspiration can be found in the literature on Initiation and the inward life, but, to really understand our ways, you are advised to seek the guidance of an experienced Brother within the Craft.

In your First Degree you laboured to ensure purity and control of your body and sense-nature. Your work in the Second Degree is to clarify your mind and discipline your thoughts. This is intellectual work, enabling you to learn to control prejudices and preconceived ideas. You are preparing your mind to approach the Truth fearlessly and to follow wherever it may lead. The discipline of the Second Degree helps you acquire mental tranquillity in the most trying or disturbing circumstances. It teaches you to control your thoughts and to closely tyle the door of your mind so that nothing enters that ought to be kept out.

By mental discipline you can secure inward peace. The mind can become an unruffled pool, a burnished mirror, capable of reflecting without distortion the light of ultimate Truth when its Sun rises – when, as our ritual says, the rays of heaven shed their blessed and benign influence upon you.

This Degree announces the existence of a great and divine Light at our Centre. Such a discovery cannot come to a restless mind. If your mind is crowded with rushing, ungoverned thoughts, if it is fevered with business and temporal concerns, you will never find this central truth. Only in utter quiet of body and mind, and by constant meditation, will you learn to acquire the serenity to see into the Centre of life. This deeply in-seeing vision penetrates beyond appearances and surface values to simplify your concept of existence. It reduces multiplicity to unity and reveals time to be just a phase of eternity.

## The Winding Staircase

Inside the building is a winding staircase. Circular staircases have enormous symbolic value; they are passages that lead to hidden knowledge for those who ascend them.

As you learn to untangle your consciousness from material things, you can climb towards celestial planes. As you do so you will begin to understand that the Cosmic Law of the Grand Geometrician is spiral in form. Progress is made not by straight-line motion, as our senses often deceive us into supposing, but circularly, by following a tightening spiral path, progressively approaching the Truth.

The essence of Second-Degree work is scientific research. It is a mystical investigation of the abstract forces that can limit the human spirit. Recent research has discovered what our ancient Brethren well knew by more esoteric methods, that all motion is curved, and no straight lines exist in Nature. Even light bends, as the field of gravity moves it in whorls and vortices. Stellar nebulae are huge spirals of incandescent gas, and our solar system swings spirally towards a still vaster centre. This universal spiral principle is found even in tiny things – in the shape of a dust-eddy, in the shell of a snail or a whelk, the horn of a ram, the tendrils of a plant or the curl of a child's hair.

This is the truth contained in the Masonic imagery of the winding staircase. By spiral motion the human spirit issues from its primal source until it stands clothed with its present fleshy mortality. Conversely, as the spirit re-ascends, by a reverse spiral motion it casts off superfluous garments. The spirit clothes itself to come down, and divests itself to go up. When you seek the light, you symbolically divest yourself of clothing and worldly possessions that are not part of that light.

The descent of the spirit into this material world and its evolutionary re-ascent out of it is also illustrated by the symbol of the Jacob's ladder that is shown in the board of the First Degree as a great stairway, rising from the altar. The Second-Degree Board re-expresses the same truth in a more detailed way to disclose the secret of the spiral.

The spiral nature of cosmic spiritual energy can be put in plain words using an analogy. Imagine an immense double helix, a huge corkscrew, reaching from the Heavens to the Earth and rotating continually, its upper curve lit from above, its underside dark. Imagine this rotary motion sweeping downwards living spirits caught up in it, through spiral after spiral of progressive materialism, until at its base they are completely immersed in darkness. You are a spiritual being, yet you can be so drugged by the darkness of material conditions that you lose sight of your inherent spirituality. And in doing so you lose the knowledge of your true nature and spiritual secrets of your being.

Now follow the re-ascent via the reverse upward motion of this double helix. The same force that carried you down into deepening darkness will, if you co-operate with it, carry you back to increasing light. In a way it is like the escalators or moving staircases in London

Tube stations: the same force is carrying people both down into the bowels of the earth and up to the light of day.

When our minds re-ascend we shed our materialism with each successive upward twist of the spiral, until we attain complete spirituality. The level of the spiral on which we live will appear to us a closed world. Its roof will screen off our view of the plane above, its floor shut out the plane below. But each complete twist of the spiral will elevate us to a higher order of being, to a new environment, and to changed states of consciousness.

The winding staircase is a symbol of this cosmic life-process. It shows your personal path to the spiritual heights. This is why you were directed to take your steps towards the East as though mounting a spiral way. This ritual act helps you to surrender yourself to systematic meditation upon the worlds above you and the path conducting you to them.

Like the initiates of Egypt in the *Book of the Dead*, you are encouraged to say, 'I will set up my ladder that will lead me to the vision of the gods'. Climb that spiral way, and you will find the value of our symbolism justified. You will come to realise that it is possible to experience complete detachment from the world of flesh and sense and to ascend into the upper mansions of the great House of Life.

## *The Armed Wardens*

The Tracing Board shows that the upward spiral path is doubly guarded, and you will find yourself challenged and unable to ascend it unless you learn the appropriate password. Wardens stand at the foot and summit of the winding staircase to guard its access. The secrets and mysteries of higher states of being are kept from you until – morally, intellectually and spiritually – you are ready for them. The ritual insists you must be properly prepared and in possession of the password. But this password is more than a taught vocalisation. It is not a question of simply being able to utter the correct shibboleth; it is a test of merit for your whole nature. If your spirit fails to ring true, you will not be able to enter a higher state of consciousness. You will have to go back and train yourself further, until you are properly prepared.

The figure of a Sphinx was set outside ancient temples of Initiation. (One survives near the entrance to the Great Pyramid.) Egyptian legend says that if you cannot answer its test question you will not only be debarred from the Mysteries, you will also devoured or made mad.

The armed wardens posted as sentries upon the winding staircase illustrate this myth in our board. They are there to warn Candidates that admission to the knowledge of supra-physical planes is prohibited until you are properly prepared. Any attempt by unqualified minds or using illicit methods (which do indeed exist) can prove fatal to your sanity.

Let no one imagine this warning is unjustified. The average modern Mason is not often interested in states of consciousness, so he is protected from personal peril by his own ignorance of the methods known to the more experienced. It is possible to raise consciousness to abnormal levels and manipulate concealed spiritual forces within your mind to selfish ends. If in due time you come to learn something of these things, you will find within yourself powers which serve as Guardians of the Threshold who will challenge your right to enter the higher planes of life, just as the Tyler and Inner Guard challenge any intrusive stranger to the Lodge.

One of the deeper secrets of Initiation is that the way of wisdom is to wait in patience and humility till one's personal ear of corn ripens. Then by a system of right thought and living, the spirit's powers unfold into perception of worlds beyond our normal cognisance.

## The Wages

Our ritual asserts that our ancient Brethren, while building the Temple, took their wages without scruple or diffidence. It says they had complete confidence in the justice of their employer.

Why should this matter? Taken literally, this teaching about wages seems to have no practical use. But it is part of the veil of allegory in which our whole mystical doctrine is clothed. We need to draw that veil aside and look at the body beneath it.

When you set your feet upon a path towards the Light of the East and enter the Porchway to deeper knowledge, when you mount the winding stairway to the heights, then you make a break with your past. You put your old order of life behind you, detach yourself from your previous interests and move towards something better. You begin to reconstruct your life and adapt it to new ideals.

The light of a great promise shines before you, and you can experience a joy such as you have never before known. But you will find that the world and your old life will not readily let you go. You are part of your past, and your old ways will not easily be uprooted. You might find your family and close friends turning against you, wondering at the change that has come over you. Sickness, business upsets or financial losses, unexpected hammerings of fate, trouble in any of its many forms, may assault you just as you feel you are within reach of better things. You may find yourself oscillating between states of light, joy and exaltation, and periods of darkness, dismay and profound depression.

You will find yourself asking: 'How is it that these things happen to me just as I have seen a glimpse of true light and begun to walk the path of real progress? Is that light after all but a will-o'-the-wisp? Is that path really true and worthwhile?'

You must expect experiences of this kind. They are the wages referred to in the ritual. You have to learn to accept them without complaining, without scruple or diffidence. The fact that you receive them, good or bad, is evidence of your spiritual progress. So long as you remain comfortably stagnant in your old life and swim with the current of the outer world, you are self-contented but spiritually asleep. The moment you wake from this stupor and try to swim against the current, you stir up adverse energies from your past. You cause reactions from within yourself. Effects that, under other circumstances, would have worked themselves out more slowly, come to dominate your mind.

These are what is meant by your just dues. Don't be dismayed at them; be thankful to balance your account with the Moral Law. Nothing can come to you, whether agreeable or unpleasant, except as the fruits of your past actions. Whatever occurs to you, joyous or painful, is either a reward due to you or a debt due from you. These experiences are salutary lessons in wisdom but are conducive to the fortitude and stability of spirit which you will need as you move to higher degrees of experience.

The Masonic Porchway is the threshold over which you enter the spiral to the heights. You must learn to receive your wages in the confidence that your inner centre dispenses them with unerring justice and unfailing mercy. You will learn, in humility and philosophic detachment, to stand apart from the fluctuations of outward events and personal fortune, regarding them as an almost disinterested spectator and knowing they are powerless to touch your true spiritual self: your centre. Like the ear of corn, your centre is brought to ripeness not just by benign sunshine, but also by storms of wind and rain. You move from a white square to a black and from a black to a white, with your character forming as you respond to each.

These remarks may help you see why this Second Degree is called one of passing. It is a transitional point, a midway stage in the process of the spirit's Initiation into the ultimate secrets and mysteries of being. Its aim is to induce you to expand and illuminate your mind by intellectual and meditative exercises. This work takes you farther than the preparatory control of the bodily senses and moral virtues laid down in the First Degree. Yet, even when the skill of a Fellowcraft Mason is achieved, its rewards remain inferior to those that you will ultimately attain in the Sublime Degree of Real Initiation yet to come.

Masonic allegory is a veil of enduring truth. It is not just a dusty storeroom of archaic symbols and obsolete forms, but a helpful expression of a doctrine valid in all ages. The emblems we have interpreted – the fall of mystical cleansing water, the ear of golden grain, the sheltering porch, and the guarded stairway circling up into concealed Truth – have all in the past served to assist intellectual and spiritual development. And they can assist us today, since the realities they symbolise have not changed. Nor will they change while the world endures and the temple of the perfected human spirit is incomplete.

May this outline of the Second Degree help to you to plant the seed of our symbolic system in your mind and grow a blade of personal knowledge about its vital truths. Let it shape your intellect into acceptable material to build the Great Architect's world-temple and help you aspire to become a perfected Living Stone.

# CHAPTER FIVE

# THE THIRD MASONIC STEP TO INITIATION

When you approach the Third, or Sublime, Degree properly prepared, it is presumed you will have left the outer world far beneath you. You will have risen above the mental levels of the First and Second Degrees. You will have symbolically ascended into the solitude and rarefied atmosphere of a mountaintop. But watch out, because mountaintops are places where you are liable to find yourself enveloped in cloud and darkness.

Our ritual makes that darkness visible in the silence of the Lodge. It is the purpose of the dark reflective silence which knowledgeable lodges use just before and just after moments of high ritual importance. If you study records of mystical experiences you will see that this ritual gloom is described as the Divine Dark. It represents a state higher than that of reasoning thought, a state of obscurity and difficulty that the human mind must enter and pass through before reaching light and glory beyond.

The light of the centre is always first perceived as darkness visible, because our perceptive faculty is not attuned to it. But we see dark only because we can not cope with excessive brightness.

The Third Degree deals with a subject that is not capable of simple explanation. If parts of our ritual seem dark and abstruse, this is because their subject matter is not drawn from the level plains of everyday knowledge but from the peaks of human experience.

The First Degree is concerned with the discipline of the body, and the Second with the culture of the mind, but the Third deals with the awakening of the spirit. It must be interpreted from the spiritual plane and by the light of the spirit. It makes no sense from any lower level of understanding.

## THE SUBLIME DEGREE

At first sight the Tracing Board of the Third Degree may seem simple, but it is the most cryptic of all, and heavily charged with meaning. Its simplicity masks profundity, but its message is difficult because it deals with matters in which few care to interest themselves.

Our three Degrees stand for three time-honoured stages in philosophic mysticism:

First, that of *Purification*, involving the discipline and control of the objective sense-nature.

Second, that of *Illumination*, which occurs after the application of similar discipline and control to the subjective mental nature.

These lead to the stage of *Perfection*, our third Sublime Degree of mystical death and resurrection. This is a crucial regenerative event that raises you above the normal human mystical level and lets you take a great step forward in the evolution of your spirit. You become an Initiate, a Spiritual Adept, a Master Mason.

This is fully pictured in the Third-Degree Tracing Board (see Plate 3), which serves as a hieroglyphic figure embodying secrets of wisdom and instructions for the realisation of the principles of the Degree. But first let me explain what the board shows.

Whichever form of board is used, the main reference is to Hiram Abif. Sometimes it bears words in cipher that, when decoded, relate to him and yield the reputed date of his death; sometimes it shows the faint outline of his concealed body. Other details of the board are explained in our ordinary Ritual, and I do not need to repeat that teaching here. If you are a Master Mason you already know it; if you are not, it will mean nothing to you. But the official explanation that we work in Lodge is only a superficial part of the general veil of allegory in which the real doctrine of the Craft is shrouded. It is this ulterior significance of the Degree that I am seeking.

# THE TRADITIONAL HISTORY

Our ritual tells the Masonic legend of Hiram Abif. There is no historical or scriptural support for this narrative, indeed the Craft legend conflicts with the Biblical details of the building of the Temple and its architect. The Bible states that 'Hiram made an end of building the temple,' which was then consecrated and used; our legend declares that it remained incomplete, because of his untimely death and the loss of The Plan. The Bible also makes no mention of Hiram's death, by murder or otherwise.

So our Craft legend of Hiram Abif is pure myth. But myth is not irresponsible fiction: it is an ancient and effective way of conveying truths about life to the receptive and properly prepared mind. Our legend, though called a traditional history, would be better described as an historical tradition. It is a form of cosmological doctrine expressed in numerous forms by humans since the beginning of time. It puts forward guidelines to explain the genesis, fall, and destiny of mankind. And it explains why our world is afflicted by evil, sin and death. The myth begins as a primal tragedy, the murder and burial of the Master-builder Hiram Abif.

This mythical truth was taught by imagery among all the nations of antiquity. We find it in one of the oldest of the Mysteries, the Samothracian, where the murder appears as the tragedy of a god slain by his fellow gods. Its equivalent in Egypt is the legend of the murder of Osiris by Set. In Greece it appears in the dismemberment of Dionysus by the Titans and his concealment in a secret place. In Phoenicia it is told as the murder of Adonis, in the Norse sagas as the death of Baldur. Ancient British tradition echoes it in the story of King Arthur, wounded and mysteriously concealed through the ages but destined to return, and the Germanic legend of the Nibelungs, the murder of Siegfried and fall of the gods is another variation on the same theme.

Each of these myths – not to mention the story recorded in the Christian Gospels – tells of a great and blameless being, a divine or semi-divine master or worker for human good, who is opposed and done away with by certain rebellious ruffians, Titans or Giants. These typify the crude and hostile blind forces of Nature. The loss of the mythical hero temporarily checks the advance of human progress. But the hero re-emerges from concealment, restores what has been lost, and so re-establishes the fortunes of humanity.

With each case of a murdered or smitten Master one finds a cavern, tomb or sarcophagus, used as a place of burial or concealment. It is from this grave that the hero will rise again. Usually there is a reference to some object – often a plant, as a symbol of growth – placed upon it to mark its site. In Greek myth a branch of olive planted to mark a cavern in the *Odyssey*. In the Egyptian version a tamarisk plant located the grave of Osiris, as the acacia did that of Hiram, while a red anemone showed where the blood of Adonis was spilt. Virgil, an initiate of the Mysteries of Isis who knew the doctrine from that source, repeats it in describing how Aeneas discovered the body of the demigod Polydorus by accidentally pulling up a loosely planted shrub.

In the Craft legend of the murder and loss of the building plan, we have a retelling of a doctrine of cosmic tragedy affecting all humanity. When the builder is smitten all Nature groans and is cast into travail. Because of this loss, human society is in a state of disorder and confusion. Few members of our Craft realise that, in giving the sign of horror, they are testifying to this cosmic calamity. It is really a sign of dismay for the tragic results of an original sin, while the sign of sympathy is similarly an expression of personal contrition for it. When giving these signs we identify with the force of this myth.

This ruinous loss and its cyclical renewal, is the *raison d'être* of the secret Mystery schools and their present day agent, the Craft. For all those systems, including Masonry, were instituted for the sole purpose of asserting the truth of the spirit's fall into material darkness and its restoration to light. They also provide a means by which the spirit may become purified and redeemed. All these myths presuppose that humanity can know a state of perfection and that it has become unhinged and uncentred from its true root of being. They also offer various means of restoration to perfection, including secret knowledge and perfecting rituals.

In this way a cosmic mystery is reduced to a personal mystery. So a route to a personal spiritual perfection is taught by our Craft system.

## The Personal Mystery

There is a uniform course of action behind all Initiation systems. First there is a course of physical and mental training, corresponding to the work of our First and Second Degrees. This then leads to a Third-Degree ritual of Death and Rebirth.

Having first brought you to the prime of your physical and mental powers, The Craft will then offer you this Sublime Degree and call upon you to undergo a crucial trial to lift your spirit to a far higher state. It does not involve the physical end of your bodily life, but it does involve the permanent death of your unregenerate ego. If you successfully endure the trial you will vastly increase your spiritual stature. This experience will endow you with the knowledge, powers and qualities of a Master.

After purification and preparation there follows your last and greatest trial. It is a ceremony of the utmost solemnity and secrecy in which you lie entranced in the grave. After passing through this intense spiritual state you are restored, as a spirit raised on the Five Points of Fellowship. In our ritual we refer to rising from the Tomb of Transformation.

The methods of the Initiating Officers and the nature of the experience itself must be lived out to understand its effect. No one ever understands without experiencing it. No one ever participates in this ritual except those who have already undergone it, and so can apply their own understanding to help you to your desired result. It is an experience in which your consciousness is withdrawn and rendered dead to all earthly concerns. It is introverted and directed backwards through psychic darkness towards the Centre – the source and root of all being – and there your mind passes into union with the light of the cosmic Centre, which is the source and inspiration of your personal spirit. It is an experience which either finds you in a state of sanctity or leaves you in one.

This sublime event forces you to a conscious awareness of your mortality. It establishes a union between your human spirit and the cosmic principle. By reknitting your lower carnal personality with your centre (your higher self or spiritual principle), you become perfected. After this experience you will be an Initiate Master, whose cornerstone is finally placed in its true position.

It is difficult to convey the reality underlying this ritual in mere words. Indeed, its significance is not always understood by the majority of those who perform it. We need among us more expert Master Masons qualified to undertake the solemn responsibility involved. And to this end it is desirable that we understand exactly what our Third Degree implies.

The public literature upon so secret a subject is scanty, not only because of the Craft's tradition of secrecy, but because any explanation of the process of Initiation is meaningless until you take part and are changed by the process. But the earnest non-Masonic enquirer will find plenty to meet the basic knowledge of the words and stage directions in the ritual books of the Craft, which are freely available.

Of the ritual of the ancient mysteries, the best-known instances are to be found in the Egyptian *Book of the Dead*. And in the *Alcestis* Euripides alludes to what occurred in the Orphic and Eleusinian rites. He speaks about entering the grave and returning therefrom, regenerated, on the third day Virgil speaks of it in the sixth book of the *Aeneid*, describing Aeneas passing through Hades into Elysium and there finding his paternal spiritual principle, his dark journey being lit only by the Golden Bough: the glimmering ray of his own spirit. Dante's *Divine Comedy* is another poetic account of passing through the underworld via a purifying plane to paradise beyond, and the walk through the Valley of the Shadow of Death in the 23rd Psalm is one of many Biblical allusions to it. For Master Masons this psalm is a constant reminder of their own Raising Ceremony and its perambulations in darkness, under constant tests of fortitude, guided only by the intuitive spark of their own spirit. Only when you have been symbolically drawn into union with your Master-principle, is that darkness dispersed by an influx of dazzling light.

Our Third-Degree ceremony can be compared to that great poetic drama of Initiation, the Book of Job. There you will find described the stripping of the Candidate's entire worldly possessions, the tests, trials and ordeals to which his old self must be subjected, the drying up of all the springs and desires of the natural man until the fire of his sensuous life is reduced to a heap of ashes. There, too, you will read of his steadfast cleaving to his sole remaining glimmer of intuitive light, despite subtle efforts to weaken his will and divert his attention from the path. At length a supernal Light breaks onto him in its glorious fullness. At long last the Initiate knows that a redeeming principle lives in him and that – whilst in his flesh, yet apart from it – he has seen the Most High. Lastly you see him restored to his material comforts and the companions of his former toils. Job has all his former worldly possessions restored to him, now multiplied exceedingly because of the new and enhanced value they take on in the light of the new consciousness he has attained

## WHO WAS HIRAM ABIF?

Who was Hiram Abif, and why were you identified with him by being made to represent him?

It was the practice of the old colleges of Initiation to identify the Candidate with some ideal hero. This prototype would be a person who had passed through the ordeal of dying to the old life and been raised or reborn to the new. This archetype would have trodden every step of the painful path and could therefore serve as an exemplar to others seeking the same goal.

Had you been initiated in Egypt you would have stood in for Osiris. In Greece, it would have been Dionysus or Iacchos. In Persia, you would been Mithras. If you entered a medieval Order of Christian Chivalry you would, like Parsifal, have followed the way of the Cross until it brought you to the Holy Grail. If you took Rosicrucian Initiation, you travelled with Father Christian Rosycross until, like him, you slept the death-sleep in the House of the Holy Spirit. All these systems express a common truth in different ways and lead to the same goal. But our Craft is expressed in terms of Hebrew mysticism, and our prototype is the Chief Architect and Master-builder appointed by King Hiram of Tyre to erect a temple for King Solomon.

These three mythical characters, two Hirams and a Solomon, combine to symbolise a threefold creativity. *Wisdom* (represented by Solomon, king of Israel) has the vision to create. *Strength* and resources, personified by Hiram, king of Tyre, project the world of Nature, as the material out of which creative ideas take shape in our minds. Architectonic and geometrical power finally moulds that idea into the *Beauty* of objective form, and Hiram Abif personifies this third aspect of creative energy. He represents the Cosmic Builder; the Great Architect by whom all things are made. This great trinity is symbolised by the equilateral triangle, often placed within the circle, to represent the completed Initiate.

The name Hiram Abif – sometimes given as Adoniram – is the Hebrew form of the Greek Hermes. Hermes was the son of the All-Father (Zeus) and the messenger and intermediary between the gods and men. His role was to show men how to live and give them safe conduct through death. In Greco-Alexandrian scriptures he is called both Hermes and Thoth (the Divine Thought or Creative Mind) and appears as the great Initiator and Teacher of hidden knowledge. Hermes is also mentioned in some of the old Masonic charges. Modern Masons, who honour Hiram Abif as their Grand Master and exemplar, would profit enormously by studying the large body of Hermetic (Hiramitic) literature available. This includes the great treatises upon initiation: *The Divine Pymander of Hermes Mercurius Trismegistus*, G.R.S. Mead's great studies entitled *Thrice-Greatest Hermes*, and *The Shepherd of Hermas*, the latter a work of inspired instruction to mystical Masonry.

Hiram Abif is not a man, he is an archetype. He is an exemplar and revealer – like Orpheus, Osiris, and Jesus – who re-expresses the virtues of each of these great prototypes. All these archetypes reveal truth to a fallen world and help benighted humanity find the light. They were all said to go about doing good and teaching men how to rebuild the fallen temple of the spirit. All met with hostility from envious ruffians, since their teaching was contrary to the ways of the world. All were slain by those they sought to save. All rose above death to a higher order of life. Once risen, they were in spiritual touch with their disciples and helped them on their way. The uniform tragedy of their lives is accounted for by the fact that each is an echo of a primal spiritual tragedy which every mind senses. It is this sense of separateness and isolation that ruptures the spirit's cosmic harmony and explains the chaos and confusion of human existence.

Our ritual speaks of the sound of lamentations and regrets sounding from a deep cave after the Master's death. That cavern symbolises our material world. The sounds are the cries of the world's pain, illustrating the groans and travail of Nature waiting for redemption. Our myth tells of the misery of a race that knows there is a golden age to be enjoyed, yet lives in darkness. Our spirit is exiled in a strange land, but a subliminal impression of light lingers in us. The ritual reproduces popular mythologies and scriptures of the past. Examples are Demeter mourning her lost child, the grief of the widowed Isis for her husband, temple prostitutes wailing for Tammuz, Rachel weeping for her children – and all refuse to be comforted.

So, as we follow the method of antiquity in our Third Degree, the cosmic mystery of the Fall and the Lost Word is brought home to us individually. It becomes our personal mystery. This Degree tells us that we are beings fallen away from our true Centre, then tells how the Centre may be restored. Its teaching gives us hope, maintaining that which is lost may be found.

The Third Degree reveals a path to return to the Centre. But it involves the death of your personal ego. It is not the death of the body, which will happen in any event in the course of nature, but a dying down of the egoistic spirit that animates that body. This egoist self is unreal, temporal and illusory, because it identifies with things of sense and mortality; it is unconscious of ulterior reality. The whole lesson of our Third Degree is that, if you are prepared to forgo this unreal self, you will make space for your true immortal self to take its place in you. Nature abhors a vacuum, and when the earthly mind of the old Adam is driven out, the quickening spirit of the new Adam fills its place.

## THE THIRD-DEGREE TRACING BOARD

The Third-Degree Tracing Board (see Plate 3) is a diagram that contains many truths. Like every effective symbol, it is capable of several meanings, each one true upon its own level.

Its first and simplest meaning is the quasi-historical one you acted out in the ritual. It shows the grave of the murdered Hiram and the tools that killed him.

Secondly, it has a cosmic and philosophic meaning. At this level it is a visual metaphor for the spiritual mystery of the origin of evil and death. This is an important and interesting meaning but is not relevant to this book.

Thirdly, it has a personal application. It is a symbol of ourselves and shows the traditional way of being raised from darkness to light. It is in this personal sense that I will analyse it.

It comprises three main features:

1. A tomb and a shroud.

2. A sprig of acacia at the head of the grave, not in true alignment with the body interred in it, but planted to one side of it.

3. Working Tools or Implements of Destruction scattered around the grave.

The grave, depicts not only the tomb used for the ritual of Initiation, but represents the darkness of your human personality. That physical body is one of darkness and mortality. As Socrates said of it, we are walking graves, carrying our tomb about with us as an oyster does its shell.

When you advanced to the East in this Degree you stepped over an open grave. This signified that you trampled your bodily nature underfoot, making it your servant instead of simply giving in to its demands.

Into that material body is infused a spirit. It is the psychic principle that elevates your animal nature to become a rational being. In the board the spirit is indicated by a chevron or triangle, with its apex pointing westwards. This indicates the downward fall of the spirit into darkness.

Your Master Mason's apron displays three rosettes, also arranged as a triangle, but with its apex up. That triangle of rosettes on the white apron is the converse of the triangle on the black grave. They mark the progress the spirit of a Master Mason has made to being raised from a fallen and dark condition to an upright, pure one. They show that what was sown as bare grain in the body of death has, by dying there, been quickened and sprung into new life. It is bearing fruit as a Master Mason, and the former wilderness is blossoming as a rose.

The rosettes on the apron represent, not only the soul, but also physiological centres. These are focal points of whirling energy that manifest at different parts of the nervous system as the soul's vitality increases and expands. Think of your four-square white apron as typifying the body purified and redeemed from deadness. The three rosettes budding from it are symbols of the spirit energising and unfolding its powers from within. The four and the three combine to make seven, the number of perfection.

The tomb is sometimes shown as a temple, because your personality is a temple to the mystery of the Centre. It is where you must serve as a high priest. That temple's chequered floor-work represents the perpetual dualism that pervades natural existence. It shows all the opposites and contrasts of good and evil inevitable to the flesh, all of which the high priest has to walk upon (in the sense of keeping them underfoot), treating them as equal in value but rising above their dualism.

The glimmer of the Bright Morning Star enters the darkness of the Lodge and illuminates the emblems of mortality via the Lodge's dormer window or roof-light. Why should our Ritual lay stress on a dormer in preference to any other window? For the same reason that a properly built Masonic Lodge has no side windows, only a roof-light. What is implied is that, whilst we are pursuing the path to the Centre, the light for that path must come from above. It symbolises the light of the heavens reaching down to our own intuitive spirit, not the sidelights of carnal reason or worldly wisdom.

The priesthoods of various religions wear a tonsure or shaven top to the head. For them the tonsure expresses the same idea as our dormer window. It is a reminder to the priest to keep his head or intellect ever open to inspiration and illumination from above.

## The Sprig of Acacia

Beyond body and mind, abides the spirit, the higher principle that affiliates you to the cosmic centre. This is represented by a sprig of acacia, planted at the head of the grave. This symbolises your supreme life-principle, from which all your subordinate faculties issue. This is the Centre, the proton around which your personal characteristics move as electrons. It is the ultimate core of your being, beyond time and space, and beyond death and evil. It is your Master-light that never goes out, even when your Lesser Lights fail. It is your star in the East or five-pointed Morning Star. If you endure to the end, the ritual promises you union with it.

In antiquity this starry principle went by many names. It has been called the Golden Branch or Golden Bough. In the Hebrew Temple it was symbolised by the Seven-branched Golden Candlestick. It is an emblem of the Tree of Life, of which each of us is a branch. It shows that we all share a common sap or life-essence from a parent trunk. It shows the quantum entanglement implicit in the Great Singularity of Creation.

The sprig is not planted directly over the head of the body in the grave, but a little to the North. It hovers over the head, but not in exact alignment with it. This detail indicates that in our present imperfect state our personality is not in true alignment with our spiritual principle: mentally, morally and physically we are out of plumb with our Centre. This is signified by the whispered secret words of this Degree, in uttering which we proclaim to one another beneath our breath that the master-principle of our being has been cut off from us, that the builder has been smitten. It reminds us that us are not in true alignment with our own chief cornerstone or central spirit, which is marked by the acacia at the head of the grave.

### *The Implements of Destruction*

A great irony lies in the fact that the Tools that slew the Master and served to bring about his destruction are the same Tools which we must use to reconstruct our fallen temple. The simple truth thus conveyed is that evil is misapplied good, and good transmuted evil. From our errors we may learn wisdom and return to grace by the correct use of that which involved us in disgrace.

The Implements point to the means by which we can get back into true alignment with our spiritual principle.

They consist of:

1. The Plumb-rule of uprightness applied to all parts of our being: *viz.*, the senses, the emotions and the mind.

2. The Level of 'equality', by which those parts (which in most people are very unequally balanced) must be brought into a condition of harmony and equilibrium.

3. The heavy Maul of a strong and resolute purpose, which nothing shall deflect from the end in view.

Few of us realise what disordered beings we are. We fail to appreciate what labour is needed to bring our personality into line with our true axis. Often our sense-nature is uncontrolled, our emotions ungoverned, or our mind undisciplined and incapable of concentration. All these parts have to be squared and brought into harmonious function in the perfect cube or finished ashlar. Only when this work is complete can the central spirit shine through them as a single perfect instrument. Hence the Craft insists upon uprightness. Not merely moral straightness and personal righteousness, but physical rectitude. You are expected to stand perfectly erect, we tell the Candidate. No sagging limbs, no lax gestures of indolence or indifference. You stand with your body erect, every aspect taut and angular, every muscle and nerve tense. Why should this be?

Physical tension, emotional control and mental concentration are valuable aids to bringing body and mind into direct alignment with your higher spiritual self. That immortal spiritual self is always upright, true and perfect. It is your lower personality that is crooked, that needs to be made straight and erect and to be brought into alignment, even at the cost of suffering to yourself. To reach the Centre you may have to face up to personal pain.

Every Initiate the world over is taught the practical value of bodily posture when engaged in the work of self-perfecting. Our Craft expressly calls for erectness, but few Brethren see, or trouble to think, why. They imagine our Masonic postures and signs are intended to be used only in Lodge as ceremonial salutes or for the purpose of recognition between Brethren. This is a great error.

The postures and signs are for private use also. As a real Initiate, when you meditate in private, you should tyle the door both of your chamber and your mind, stand to order as a Mason and maintain the sign of the Degree in which you desire to open the Lodge of your spirit. Then meditate and perform other Masonic labour in a condition of physical uprightness and mental tension, holding your body in the posture of Masonic alertness. This promotes the alignment, co-ordination and harmony of your mind, emotions and body with your centre. The posture itself becomes an offering up of yourself to be made perfect in all your parts. It is an act of true self-building, the value of which will only be learned by experience, but it is perhaps no easy task for novices to square the Living Stone. It is, however, something that should be attempted.

## THE MASTER MASON

To become a Candidate for real Mastership you must cultivate a dying away of personal desire for worldly possessions and position. You must reach the stage where every mundane allurement and ambition that would divert you from the goal ceases to attract and, when offered, proves a slip. There must be voluntary sacrifice and total obliteration of your personal Ego. You must erase the sense of 'myself' as something separate from other selves and having special rights or claims of its own. You must not allow yourself to become distinct from the one Life that runs through all. Your Ego must be allowed to wither till it becomes as inert and non-reactive as a corpse. Then there will be a purifying and aligning of all the parts of your mortal nature to the Centre that, like the acacia, hovers above but to the side of your lower personality. When these three factors are present, your lower natural self will be raised into conscious union with the cosmos.

When that happens your true cornerstone is placed at the head of your personal temple and completes it. In other imagery, the acacia blooms and blossoms at the head of the grave. This means that the physical brain becomes suffused with cosmic light and enjoys a consciousness that transcends that of the normal mind as sunlight exceeds that of a candle. It is a state of consciousness denoted in art by a halo around the head. It symbolises an awakening of the spirit, which has been stifled and repressed by the self-willed energies of our circumference.

A great Master said 'Ye are all gods, and all children of the Most High', though for the moment we are fallen gods, unconscious of our latent powers and so disordered that we are unable to use them. The method and discipline of Masonic Initiation were set up to help in their awakening. In the Egyptian ritual, the title with which the Candidate was dignified as he lay in the death-sleep was the great god in the sarcophagus. There his body lay, his consciousness released from its mortal fetters, forging on through the gloom and phantasmagoria of the psychic zone, through the valley of the shadow of death or divine dark, until finally he emerged into Paradisiacal Light. There at the Centre he beheld things awful and not possible to alter, things which revealed the inherent potentialities in him. Then he came back, holding this knowledge. His consciousness returned to its mortal frame, and he came forth from the Tomb of Transformation a changed man, a sanctified Initiated man. He had known life and passed through death, and so knew the secrets and held the keys of both. He was one for whom all things became new, with meat to eat and work to do that lesser men knew nothing of.

Every Initiate has to experience the supreme ordeal of passage through the Divine Dark. You must cross this unstable psychic region before you can find the light of light; all the great illuminates underwent this test. With your presiding officers, you enter a darkened Lodge and move through a symbolic nebulous underworld, guided only by the glimmer of your intuitive spirit. Then your Bright Morning Star rises. At first it is distant from you, but complete union with it is promised if you endure the last and greatest trial to its end.

This is the Degree of Death, not physical death but mystical death. It is where the Craft, after first teaching the spirit's involution into mortality and its intricate windings in that condition, finally teaches it how to die out of them. In doing so it breaks free of thraldom. You become a real Master Mason when you make that great act of self-denial, when you die that death, and experience its transformation.

You remain in the flesh until, in the course of nature and physical law, your outer casket falls away, but you no longer value the life that others cling to, or treasure the things that they prize. You transcend and outgrow them. You will feel no dread of death, for you have already been to its other side. You have seen what lies beyond, and know it to be the inevitable complement to life. It is an incident of existence like falling asleep when tired. You have risen above the dualism of life and death, joy and pain, and known Absolute Being, in which these opposites merge and find their synthesis, resolution and rest.

You can balance your pillars and become established in strength. Having lain in the Tomb of Transformation, the grave of the temporal self loses its sting, and neither bodily nor mental death can have further victory over you. Having died to yourself, the root of egoism, of sorrow, of personal ambition, and of every selfish desire at the expense of others, also withers. You will know infinity and live from the Centre.

As a Master Mason you are not easily recognised, save by your peers. Your secrets can be imparted only to those of equal rank with yourself, for only they will understand you. Was not the Temple built without the sound of axe and hammer? So does the Master Mason build. You will have to work on your spirit using working tools designed for the spirit. Nothing is more silent, yet nothing more potent. They need no visible activity, yet their use truly helps society by secret unrecognised forms of labour where the axe of self-assertion and the hammer of personal egotism are never heard.

The Third Degree we work is a faint yet faithful shadow of a sublime and sacred spiritual mystery. If natural birth and death be events to which privacy and seclusion are accorded, how much more must secrecy attach to the ultra-natural transition involved when a spirit seeks to pass through mystical death and to be reborn from the Centre?

The truths of this Degree are such that not all are ready to receive them. They are truths that cut sharply across the world's wisdom and its comfortable popular ideas. Official science and academic learning ignore them because they are unpalatable. They can even be offensive to those in whom the fever of natural life burns strongly and whose material interests are all-absorbing. Few are yet willing to let everything go and die to all that they know and care for. The whole trend of the world-spirit and conventional life supports them in their refusal.

But those who do not yet care for these truths will be brought to face them, for denial and death of the ego is the inescapable law of our progress. Life itself is a vast Initiation process, slowly, patiently leading an intractable world from darkness to increasing light.

You can choose to help this process or retard it. The Initiate is one in whom it has become accelerated. You no longer live for yourself, but to facilitate progress in others. Your desire for eating husks and chasing shadows leaves you. You forsake the shining but deceptive pillar of prosperity, suffer at the sombre whipping-post of adversity, and learn something of the meaning of our two great pillars of Boaz and Jachin. You learn to match their stability and good sense within your Lodge.

At last life confronts you with something that forces your eyes wide open and makes you desire once and forever to forsake all else and leave the West and go to the East. If you aspire to that moment these secrets of Initiation become living truths. Our ritual says that patience and perseverance will in due time entitle worthy Masons to participate in the mysteries. But, to become alive, those mysteries must be rooted in personal experience. They are difficult truths – difficult to grasp even notionally at first. They are not truths for the easy chair, or that can be the subject of platitudes and suave sentiment. Our secret lore is given only to those who sweat for it – remember that one of the signs of this Degree teaches you that to realise these truths may cost you blood and sweat. Only personal labour can awaken their truths within you, and personal experience alone will verify them. Not a thousand lectures or books will impart them. Although such aids can be useful as pointers and stimulants, they are things of the circumference addressed to a mind that is also of the circumference. It is the awakening of the Centre that brings true Initiation.

This must be striven for with a persistent determination of will and intense desire. Not all the books in the British Library can teach you what you will know conclusively and permanently at the moment the Blazing Star at your Centre dawns for an instant above your horizon, and the sprig of golden-bloomed acacia blossoms in your brain. Light from that source differs totally, both quantitatively and qualitatively from every other light that you have ever known.

# CHAPTER SIX

# THE FOURTH MASONIC STEP TO INITIATION

In certain lodges in Yorkshire the impressive Old York working still survives. In this pure form of ancient Masonry there are three other Working Tools beyond those taught in the Three Degrees. They formerly belonged to the now discarded Past Master's Degree or Degree of Installed Master. These tools were presented and explained to a new Master of a Lodge on his Installation, with Brethren below that rank kept ignorant of them.

A vital part of the Old York tradition of the Installed Master's Degree is the three Working Tools of the Initiate Lodge Master:

The first of these tools is a Plumb-line – a cord held by the fingers, with a plummet at the lower end – which enables the Master to determine the uprightness of a stone or building. On the walls of the old Lodge Room at York, where once the Grand Lodge of England met, you can still see the biblical reference to the use of the Plumb-line in Amos 7: 7–8.

The second tool is a Trowel, an implement for spreading mortar. In its symbolic sense the Initiate Master uses it to spread the cement of love among the members of the Lodge and bind them as Living Stones into unity.

The third and most significant tool is the Plan, which shows emblematic designs to guide the Initiate. It is a symbolic blue-print of the Great Architect's plan for building a Temple of perfected Humanity. The Plan is complex to understand and only given to those qualified to grasp it and assist in carrying it out.

The Plumb-line forms a vertical line; the Trowel involves a lateral horizontal spreading movement; and the two in combination form a cross: + or the Hebrew tau cross ⊤.

The tau is on every Past Master's apron, and every newly installed Master of a lodge is invested with this badge. If you wear it, that implies you know its meaning. Even more, it implies that you should be able to use it.

Its component lines are exhibited separately in the two columns on the Wardens' pedestals, one of which is always erect and the other horizontal, although their relative positions change when working or resting. But no column appears on the Master's pedestal. Why? Because when you become Master you become the synthesis of the Wardens' columns. You combine their properties in yourself. The Master is a living cross, and therefore you wear the sign of the cross upon your clothing.

In discussing the symbol of a cross I am not entering into a religious discussion or implying Christian links; I deal with the philosophical conception of the cross. This tradition dates from long before the founding of Christianity. It is taught in the mysteries of both the East and the West through the ages and is perpetuated in our system.

Plato wrote about the ancient secret doctrine. He taught that the world is built upon the principle of the cross. It is a manifestation resulting from the conflict of two opposed principles, spiritual and material, that symbolically resolve themselves into a unity that transcends dualism. In the same way, the Master absorbs the functions of his two subordinate Wardens and transcends them. To take up one's cross is to engage in the work of resolving the crux of life by reducing your spiritual and non-spiritual elements into balance and harmony. This is the great work of Masonic labour in its highest sense. As the Master of a lodge, as you achieve it in yourself, you become qualified and able to help in the task of world-building. And as a Master of the Secret Science you will discover ways to employ the symbol of the cross for many purposes in connection with constructive and beneficent work to be done in secret.

You are entrusted with the Plumb-line so that you may become a skilled tester and rectifier of the spirits of those committed to your charge. And to use it well you need to be conscious of your own spirit as the end of a silver cord running out from the light of the hidden Centre.

The Trowel you should use to spread the cement of love among your fellows. Your own spirit will become a burning centre of love, so that its radiance subtly welds others into unity, knits their separated persons into an inseparable group spirit and makes them be of one mind. In short your task is to meld them into The Perfect Lodge – a matter I will return to later.

Lastly we come to the Plan. This Working Tool makes you privy to the secret counsels of the Centre; through it you are encouraged to become a co-worker with the Most High and work with the Sacred Law of the cosmos. How can the chance to use such a Tool fail to cause the deepest sense of awe?

These tools are emblems that give a completeness and final point to the whole series of Masonic Working Tools. They add a crowning dignity and beauty to the entire structure of Craft symbolism and throw a strong beam of light upon the purpose of Initiation. The way of the Initiate leads you, first, from darkness to light, and then from light to active collaboration with the Centre. This is your creative work of building a new heaven and a new earth. Masonry, being 'a progressive science', uses progressive Working Tools, of which these three are the most advanced. As you move progressively through the Five Kingdoms of the spirit, so you learn the use of the appropriate spiritual working tools.

If these advanced tools were more widely known, that would go far to counteract the false idea that Installation in the Chair of Solomon is an accolade for the new Master of the Lodge. It would dispel the idea that the Office is due by virtue of seniority, routine or popularity, or because he has been an efficient officer and good at ritual. Prospective occupants of the Chair would see that they were placed in it not for their own or their lodge's glory. They are not there to make a great feast for themselves and their friends. Their role as Initiated Masters is to advance the cosmic work of building a better world.

Masonic Tools do not merely express abstract ideas; they are implements for doing practical work. How, then, do you use these tools? What sort of work can you perform with them. That is a matter for your own spiritual reflection and meditation, but a hint can be given.

There are three important points to remember:

1.  The use of the Tools is to bring about the conquest of
    your lower nature using the powers of your higher nature
    and spiritual will. If you are not master of your lower
    faculties then you cannot function on higher levels or
    understand the nature of cosmic work. 'He who is faithful
    in small things shall become ruler over great things.'

2.  The use of the Tools is progressive and is disclosed as you
    advance. It is hopeless to try to grasp the more advanced
    Tools, those of the Third Degree and of an Initiate Master
    until using the First- and Second-Degree Tools has become
    a habit of your life.

3.  The First-Degree Tools give a method for you to control
    your animal urges. The Second-Degree Tools show you
    how to manage your mental life. They include forms of
    abstract thought, not necessarily religious but tools of
    meditation, prayer, and mind-control. Their use leads you
    to perceive supra-mental truth and illuminate your lower
    mind. The Third-Degree Tools are for those whose
    consciousness has become raised above the life of
    common reason and everyday events. They open the way
    to the secrets of the Master's Chair and the Working Tools
    of that Office.

The Plan is the supreme Working Tool of Masonry. It is the last tool
you will learn from the ritual of the Craft. When you know the Plan
you know yourself to be part of it. You see everything around you
moving unconsciously to its fulfilment. Once you know this, your
life-difficulties are reduced. The rest is easy for the unfinished work
is frictionless and joyous. You know it to be in harmony with the
sacred law that steers the universe.

## THE TRACING BOARD OF THE CENTRE

The Plan has been represented in a Tracing Board by Bro. Wilmshurst. Plate 4 shows this Tracing Board, which is set within the boundaries of the lodge. This is to draw attention to the four symbolic directions – East, West, South and North – the symbolism of which is an important theme of Real Initiation.

The main direction of the Tracing Board runs from East at the top to West at the bottom. This is no accident, as the transition from West to East is vitally important. However, let us begin by considering the four quarters of the lodge.

The North is the side of un-enlightenment. It calls for exertion in the teeth of opposition and presents difficulties that call forth the energy of the spirit. The North is associated with mental darkness and signifies imperfection and lack of development. In olden times the bodies of suicides, reprobates and unbaptised children were always buried in the north or sunless side of a churchyard.

Junior members of the Craft are seated in the North, for, symbolically, it represents the condition of the spiritually unenlightened, the novice whose latent spiritual light has not yet risen above the horizon of consciousness to disperse the clouds of material interests and the impulses of the sensual life.

The East of the Lodge represents spirituality, the highest mode of consciousness. Often this is little developed but is still latent. It becomes active in moments of stress or deep emotion.

The West, the direct opposite of the East, represents normal rational understanding, the consciousness we employ in everyday affairs. It is material-minded and logical. Its guardian warden represents solid common sense and rational thought.

Midway between East and West is the South, the meeting-place of spiritual intuition and rational understanding. It is a point where abstract thought and intellectual power meet, to work together to accomplish the highest tasks. It is directly opposite to the North, the direction of benightedness and ignorance, controlled by sense-reactions and impressions received by our lowest and least reliable mode of perception, our physical senses.

Hence, the four sides of the Lodge correspond to four different, yet progressive, modes of consciousness: sense-impression (North), reason (West), intellectual ideation (South), and spiritual intuition (East). These make up four possible ways of knowing.

According to your development and education you tend to employ only the first two or perhaps three of these. So your outlook on life and knowledge of truth is restricted and imperfect. Full and perfect knowledge is possible only when the deep-seeing vision and consciousness of your spiritual principle has been awakened and added to your other cognitive faculties. This is possible only to the true Master, with all four methods of knowledge in perfect balance and adjusted like the four sides of the Lodge. This is why the Master and Past-Masters are placed in the East.

The personality of a Mason is made up of four basic metaphysical elements called by the ancients fire, water, air and earth. In the Tracing Board this is represented by a circle made up of four equal parts. The four parts of this circle are a reminder that the human organism is compounded of those four elements in balanced proportions. Water represents the psychic nature; Air, the mentality; Fire, the will and nervous force; whilst Earth is the material condensation in which the other three become stabilised and encased.

The circle in the centre of the tracing board represents our personal temple; and within it are four right angles, each forming the fourth part of the circle of our self:

In the North-West is the earthly body, which concentrates on the irrational demands of the flesh. It is represented by the element Earth.

The South-West is the rational mind, which can control and counterpoise the irrational body. It is represented by Air.

The South-East quarter is the emotional or psychic mind, or human consciousness, which can be swayed by both rational and irrational elements and will be influenced by whichever is allowed to predominate. It is represented by the element Water.

The North-East quarter is the spirit, a supra-rational principle capable of comprehending the transcendental nature of the unifying principle of the universe. It is shown as the element of Fire.

This Tracing Board helps us to understand the purpose of the three Degrees of the Craft. The First Degree equips us to develop a rational mind and bring our intellect (Air in the Tracing Board) into balance with the irrational urges of the flesh (shown as Earth in the Tracing Board). To aid us in this we are equipped with postures, a lodge structure to focus our thinking and a set of symbols and spiritual Tools. Only when we have balanced our rational mind against our bodily urges, learned how to how to use posture, to comprehend symbolism and gained proficiency in the use of spiritual Tools are we ready to move on the Second Degree.

The Second Degree helps us to balance our intellect (Air) and our emotions (Water) so that we learn how to recognise truth and discriminate between irrational urges of the flesh (Earth) and the truth of the spirit (Fire). We are given further postures, tools and symbols to help us strengthen our rational mind and to learn to handle our emotions so that we are prepared for the discovery of the blazing star of truth, which is as yet only visible as darkness at our Centre. Here we meet the spiral symbol, which can teach us how to approach the Centre. The postures affect our body and feed back hormonal responses into our rational minds, so helping us learn how to subdue emotion. But before we can proceed to the Third Degree we must be prepared to let go of our ego and self-regard.

In the Third Degree we allow our ego and rational mind to die, so that our spirit may be reborn as the keystone of our being and be supported in its quest to attain the vision of light which emanates from the Centre. The ritual of death and rebirth stills the urges of our body, our intellect and our emotion and brings forth the suppressed spirit. In this Degree the circle of our being is rendered complete and perfect by acquiring mastery over the harmony and balance of its four component parts. When this is fully achieved a Master of the Craft has undergone a radical transformation of the mind and a regeneration of his entire nature. Now are we ready to allow the light of the Centre to flow through fresh channels in the brain, so that the true secrets of the Craft may be internalised.

In the ritual of the Third Degree this transformation is symbolised as the Gates of Beauty, Works and Wisdom. At each gate stands an aspect of our lower self, each a traitor, seeking the secrets of the spirit for selfish ends. An intuition of right conduct arises in the Initiate's spirit and attempts to escape through the Southern Gate of Works. Our lower self, afraid that it must reform its bad habits and prune its excesses, refuses let our spirit rise free.

Now our inner wisdom tries to escape through the Western Gate of Wisdom/Knowledge. Here another aspect of the lower self resents it, afraid of the need to make fresh mental adjustments. Once more our spirit is struck down.

Finally this higher self staggers to the Eastern Gate of Beauty, where all inspiration of spiritual vitality is stifled by our lower sensual nature. Our spirit, finding its retreat cut from the outer life of the world off at the only three gates it knows, is slain and must lie in the tomb, awaiting the master light of all our seeing. We must learn to discipline those three ruffians enlisting the Principal Officers in our personal Lodge. Then, as Hiram Abif, we will be raised to become a balanced and harmonious personality, with the Blazing Star at our Centre informing all aspects of our life.

This state of Initiation is the Fifth Kingdom of nature. It is a transcendental condition of consciousness. It is within you, not of this world yet personally realisable here and now. It is a treasure, hidden in everyone's personal depths, towards which all Masons should constantly aspire. But it is a state which can only be reached with the corporate co-operation of a Lodge of Initiate Masters.

This Fifth Kingdom is not a matter of time or place but a state of consciousness. It comes like a lightning strike moving from East to West. It is like the rays of the Bright Morning Star which, in the

Masonic sense, unites our spiritual and material poles (the East representing our spirituality and the West our material and rational thinking). The tension between them is implied by placing the symbolic blazing Sun in the Centre of the Lodge to represent the light of consciousness.

As a Candidate for Initiation you are first placed in the North-East corner, where you are intended to see that on one side of you is the path that leads to the perpetual light of the East, into which you are encouraged to proceed, and on the other is that of spiritual obscurity and ignorance, in which you can remain or into which you can relapse. It is a parable of the dual paths of life open to each one of us; on the one hand, the path of selfishness, material desires and sensual indulgence, of intellectual blindness and moral stagnation; on the other, the path of moral and spiritual progress, in pursuing which you may come to decorate and adorn the Lodge within yourself with the ornaments and jewels of grace, and with the invaluable furniture of true knowledge. The mark of those jewels is that they are movable and transferable. When displayed in our own lives and natures their influence becomes transferred and communicated to others and helps to uplift and sweeten the lives of our fellows. Other jewels are immovable, because they are permanently fixed and planted in the roots of our own being, and are the raw material which has been entrusted to us to work our chaos and roughness into due and true form.

This Tracing Board shows the Lodge as an elongated (or duplicated) square, because man's organism does not consist of his physical body alone. The physical body has an ethereal counterpart in the astral body, which is an extension of the physical nature and compounded of the same four elements in an impalpable form. The oblong spatial form of the Lodge therefore symbolises the physical and ethereal nature in each of us.

During the rituals you follow a path of spiral pilgrimage around the circumference of the circle, which contains the circle of your inner self. The Tracing Board describes this path in terms of a sequence of symbols. Inspiration begins in the East with an upward-pointing equilateral triangle with a blazing light at its centre. This represents the rising of the Bright Morning Star within the Earth-based triangle of rational thought. The base of the triangle is aligned along the balance between the emotions and the intellect (Earth–Air), whilst its apex points towards the spiritual East. It suggests that there is a spiritual star shining at the centre of the rational and emotional urges of the candidate.

The path continues to the South, the area of intellect. Here there is a more complex symbol consisting of a square, a circle, two interlaced equilateral triangles and a centre. The triangles can be drawn with their apexes pointing upwards and downwards respectively. These were known in mediaeval Kabbalism as the triangles of fire and water respectively. Symbolically the triangle of fire refers to the spiritual nature, and the triangle of water to the mental or rational nature; interlaced, they show the spirit in perfect balance with the mind.

The square, triangle, circle and point, are symbols known as Platonic solids: *i.e.*, basic geometrical principles of the invisible Real and Eternal World that lies behind and controls the phenomenal and temporal world. This science of spiritual geometry reveals the true principles upon which you must build your personal temple. The Square is the symbol of the human spirit as it is generated out of the inspiration that underlies it. That spirit was created square and perfect, though invested with freedom of choice and a capacity for error. But this symbol also has, within the Square, a circle with a centre point. The circle within a Square has special significance. The Square represents the spirit as it exists in the outward Universe, symbolised by the Lodge, with its directions and their significances. As you move around the circumference you are searching for the light of inspiration which initiated your quest. If you can make contact with that central principle by a voluntary renunciation of the intervening obstructions and inharmonious elements in yourself, then you cease to be a rationalised animal and become aware of your inner links to omniscience. In this way you recover the lost and genuine secrets of your own being as you reach a point from which no Master Mason can ever err, which is the end, object and goal of your search.

The opening and closing of the Lodge in the Third Degree reveals the philosophy of the Masonic system. It says that the human spirit originated in the eternal East, in the world of Spirituality and that thence it has directed its course towards the West, the material world that is the antithesis of the spiritual. Its purpose in journeying from the spiritual to the physical is to recover what it has lost, but what, by your own industry and suitable instruction, you hope to find. What it is that has been lost is not explicitly declared, but is implied to be the genuine secrets of a Master Mason – this is the loss of the essence of your own being. In other words, your loss is the fact that your spirit has ceased to be aware of the cosmos and has become imprisoned within a limited terrestrial consciousness.

The Square shows the influence of the outside cosmos which evolved this searching spirit. The circle was used by the old Initiates to demonstrate the all-encompassing nature of the human mind. This symbol shows the candidate simultaneously as a square – finite, material and form-fettered – and yet as potentially a Circle – spiritual, infinite and free. It indicates that when the outward temporal self attains balance with the inward immortal spirit, the Square of the former becoming equal to and in equilibrium with the Circle of the latter, the Candidate's evolution is complete. Initiates now know that which makes them human. They must gradually digest the Masonic teachings in the closed circle of their own minds to extract their final values, at which point they will Square the Circle. (This is an occult expression signifying that deity, symbolised by the all-containing Circle, has attained form and manifestation in a Square or human spirit. It expresses the mystery of the Initiation within the individual spirit.)

However, inside this symbol is a triangle with its apex downwards and base upwards: an ancient symbol of the psychic constitution known as the water triangle. It is interlaced with a fire triangle, a symbol of the spirit which imparts functional energy. Of itself this spirit would be passive, a negative quantity unbalanced by a positive opposite. But by the interaction of the individual qualities of the personality, represented by the interlaced triangles, the spirit may hope to find the glory at the Centre within the Square creation of the cosmos. This symbol is first encountered in the Southern part of the Lodge, the area dominated by logic and learning. It is also found on the cusp point where the religious inclinations of the spirit (symbolised by Water) meet the rational arguments of the material mind (symbolised by Air).

Here is the point where you, the Masonic pilgrim, are forced to rationalise your longing for spiritual understanding. What do you seek? What are the Lost Secrets you hope will lead you to the brightness of the Centre, which you first glimpsed dimly through the imbalance of your emotions and rational mind. To find answers you must move on towards the West. This is the point where your emotions and reason will come into intimate contact with each other in the most material region of the lodge.

The symbol you meet at this point is a Square – but a dark, black, threatening Square. What does it mean? You are now deep in the work of the Second Degree: the education, discipline and control of your mental faculties, the gradual discovery of the secrets and mysteries of Nature and of yourself as part of Nature. You are trying to turn yourself into a true die or Square. It is at this point that your individualisation as a unitary Ego attains its climax. The Perfect Cube represents the human mind brought to perfection in the natural order. But perfection in the natural order is not your final goal; it is only a halfway house to the spiritual or ultra-natural order. When the Perfect Ashlar stage has been reached there awaits for everyone the last and greatest trial, the death prefigured by our Third Degree, involving the annihilation of all sense of the personal self, the killing of the strongly individualised Ego-consciousness. The darkness of this Square is that of death itself. This is the Valley of Death that our ritual tells us we need to travel through before we can rise and shine as the stars for ever. And the first star is visible in the fading light of the South-West corner of the Lodge.

As in the outer heavens of nature, the sun, moon and stars exist and function, so in the personal heavens of each Mason there operate metaphysical forces inherent in yourself and described by the same terms. In the make-up of each of us there exists a psychic field of various forces, determining our individual temperaments and tendencies, and influencing our future. To those forces Masonry also gives the names of Sun, Moon and planets, and the science of their interaction and working out was the ancient science of Masonic Astrology: one of the liberal arts and sciences recommended for the study by every Mason, and the pursuit of which belongs in particular to the Fellowcraft stage. Now you are prepared to meet the Five-Pointed Star as it sets in the West.

To become Initiated involves dying – not a physical death, but a moral way of dying in which the spirit, loosened from the body and the sensitive life, becomes temporarily detached and freed to enter a world of Eternal Light. In the ancient mysteries this change was brought about first by drastic preliminary disciplines, followed by a state of trance. It was done under the supervision of duly qualified Masters and Adepts who introjected the candidate's liberated spirit into its own interior principles until it could reach the Blazing Star, or Glory, at its own Centre. In the light of Darkness Visible it simultaneously knew itself and The Most High, realised their unity and the points of fellowship between them. The Five-Pointed Star, then, represents meanings that will either disclose themselves to advancing experience, or be imparted privately by a teacher to approved pupils. Until one possesses a high degree of understanding, such research is not permitted within the Craft, and this perpetuates a principle uniformly insisted on by teachers of wisdom throughout the ages. One of the greatest of these declared that where the carcase is, there are the eagles gathered together, implying that if the human personality suffers itself to become passive and emptied of its controlling principle, losing contact with the central spiritual ego appointed to dominate it, it becomes but an empty shell or carcase liable to invasion by all manner of undesirable and insidious entities. To reach the glory of the Centre you must be ready to let your ego die. But this is a dangerous process unless it is undertaken at that critical moment when the light of your Bright Morning Star is about to rise in the night sky.

If you are a candidate of strong virtue and level-headedness, and you know beforehand what you are doing and act under a competent teacher, there is no danger in venturing into these hidden paths. You can act with safety and follow the age-old ritual instruction to seekers of the Mysteries: to know, to will, to dare and to be silent.

Five upward steps lead from the First to the Second Degree. That is why we are told to lift our eyes to a bright Five-Pointed Star whose rising in ourselves brings peace and salvation. That is why it is possible to develop Five Points of Fellowship and self-identification, and why the number five recurs so prominently in our system.

Now the Masonic path leads from the fading light of the West and follows the dark inner thoughts of the dying ego towards the black ignorance of the North. Here you enter the dark night of the spirit, where you must strive for balance: first within yourself, then in your relationship with the cosmos. To symbolise this we see the symbol of the fire and the water triangles interlaced about the Centre, showing that you have balanced your mind and emotions with your urges and spiritual impulses, at which point you can fit yourself as a newly balanced individual into the rest of the world. Now the symbol you met in the South appears again. But this time you are not studying it, you are living it. It now shows your personality in balance with the cosmos, and your mind open to see the Centre, allowing you to reach a new level of consciousness. Your path is now open to the spiritual East.

As the faint light of the Bright Morning Star rises in your spiritual East you meet another symbol of balance and harmony. It is two superimposed Squares, one rotated through half a right angle. This symbolises the balance of the individual spirit set within a balanced universe. At this point you know your place in the cosmos. The Square of your spirit is merged into the Square of the cosmos, as represented by the Lodge, and you are now in a state of balance and harmony.

Finally you reach the East, and meet the final symbol of the pilgrimage. It is the Circle with the Centre, but now surrounded by two other triangles: a large upward-facing fire triangle containing a smaller downward-facing water triangle, each centred on the point which is always equidistant from the Centre. This is the point from which no Mason can err, the point of cosmic consciousness where your mind expands to understand your place in the cosmos.

There is one last item on the main part of the Tracing Board. A ladder reaching from the dark square of the West to the bright, centred triangles of the East. This is the route you can willingly travel from the darkness in the West to the light of the Bright Morning Star rising in your spiritual East.

What, then, is this Centre by which we hope to regain the secrets of our lost nature? We may reason from analogies. As the Sacred Laws are the centre of the whole universe and control it, as the sun is the centre and life-giver of our solar system and controls and feeds with life the planets circling round so at the secret Centre of individual human life exists a vital, immortal principle: the spirit. It is a point within the Circle of our own nature. In this physical world, the circle of our existence is bounded by two grand parallel lines, one representing Moses, the other Solomon that is to say, law and wisdom: the divine ordinances regulating the universe on the one hand, the divine wisdom and mercy that follow us all the days of our life on the other. Very truly, then, the Mason who keeps thus circumscribed cannot err.

Masonry is a system of philosophy that provides us with a doctrine of the universe and of our place in it. It has two purposes.

The first is to show that humans have fallen away from a high and holy Centre to the circumference or externalised condition in which they now live; to indicate that those who so desire may regain that Centre by finding the Centre in themselves, for, since The Grand Geometrician is as a circle whose centre is everywhere, it follows that a divine Centre, a vital and immortal principle, exists within each of us. By developing it we may regain our lost and primal stature.

The second purpose of Craft teaching is to declare the way by which that Centre may be found within ourselves, and this teaching is embodied in the discipline and ordeals delineated in the three Degrees. The Masonic doctrine of the Centre is, in other words, that the Kingdom of Heaven is within you.

To summarise: The first task of Masonic Initiates is to bring the forces within their own consciousness into balance (within the

Circle at the centre of the Tracing Board). At the same time, though, the forces of the cosmos – represented by the principal directions of Lodge (the pull of unthinking religious fundamentalism from the spiritual East, that of ignorant bigotry from the darkness of the North, the pull of intellectual over-analysis from the rational West and that of losing yourself in mindless labour from the warm glow of the Good Works of the South) – also have to be balanced. This is the message of harmony and balance within the Craft. Initiates must be balanced within themselves, and then at harmony with the Cosmos, as represented by the Lodge. When balanced individuals hold themselves at the mystical Centre of the opposing forces of the world, then the light of the Centre becomes clear. This is, of course, extremely difficult, but the understanding and effort involved in trying to achieve it serve to improve and benefit both the individual and Society in general.

Brethren, may we all come to the knowledge of how to open the Lodge upon the Centre of ourselves and so realise in our own conscious experience the finding of the imprisoned splendour hidden in the depths of our being. May the rising of our individual Morning Stars bring us peace and salvation.

# CHAPTER SEVEN

# THE LODGE AS A MODEL OF HUMAN CONSCIOUSNESS

How does the Craft doctrine guide us to seek the liberation of this imprisoned Centre? It does it by using the Lodge as model of human consciousness and showing us how to work together to achieve something which is greater than anything we can do alone.

A Lodge is more than an assembly of individuals. When properly formed it is an object lesson in the knowledge of yourself. The true work of the Craft – disciplining and perfecting yourself – cannot be entered upon without first understanding the detail of the many parts which make up your self. The Lodge provides a model to help you understand.

You are a threefold being. You have an outside personality, which functions in the world. This is temporal, mutable, and falls far short of expressing your real nature. In the Lodge this outer self is symbolised by the Tyler, whose place is outside the Lodge – just as the visible personality is outside the larger self which it enfolds. The Tyler has important duties to perform; so too has your personality, the external instrument of your larger inner self. That personality has mysteries of its own, which are the subject of worldly science outside the remit of the Masonic Craft. The concern of the Craft is not with the temporal, perishable elements of our being, but with our spirit. The Tyler guards that inner spirit from attacks by outside forces.

You also have an inside personality: a large psychological field called the mind. Your mind actuates the outside self, but is more subtle and complex; it bears the same relation to the outside self as the interior of the Lodge does to its exterior. The Secret Science of the Craft is directed towards developing your mind, and the Lodge is formed with the purpose of serving as a model of that sphere of psychical faculties and tendencies which we call the intellect. It shows how the discipline of the Craft may help develop us from a state of chaos to one of order and beauty. We can change from a rough ashlar to a perfect cube, and be carried from natural darkness into supernatural light. Just as the outer body can be opened for surgical investigation, so the Lodge can be opened so that we can understand the mechanism and purpose of our inner self.

But there is a third factor, beyond your outward person. A factor which joins you to the source of all being. This is your Spirit, your real self, your Centre, what we sometimes call your Soul. This Spirit has its mysteries, which can never be known until the teaching of the Craft has been assimilated both in theory and personal experience. The spirit indwells the mind, just as the mind suffuses the body; but only in the mind, once it is rectified, purified and worked, from the rough ashlar to the perfect cube, can the Centre be brought to life and consciousness. This is the work of the Craft Mason, and its achievement means Mastership. The Master of a Lodge is, emblematically, the point at which the spirit is in contact with the mind, and from which the Light from above streams into the Lodge of the Spirit, permeating and illumining all the latter's faculties and properties, and penetrating even to the external personality, of which the Tyler is the representative.

The Lodge is a model of that intermediate psychological field of mind that lies between the Spirit above and the Material below. The mind can direct its energies to either of these poles, becoming illumined or darkened, spiritualised or sensualised, according to its dominant tendencies. The open Lodge exemplifies the mind (in its various aspects of intuition, reason, and will), the emotions and the sense tendencies, all forming a community of so many Brethren who must learn not only to dwell together in unity but also to work together for the common good of the whole organism. These components are shown in the Lodge as separate entities, according to their functions in the mind. Some rule as Officers, others obey and learn. Some are active, others passive; some are fixed and stationary in their places, others mobile; for in the mind there are permanent elements and transitory features.

The Lodge, to be perfect, has seven primary Officers. These personify, broadly, the sevenfold structure of the mind, which, following the sevenfold principle in Nature, is, like a ray of light or a musical sound, prismatically resolvable into a scale of seven sub-modes. There are also seven secondary Officers. These personify not the structure but the activities of a mind that has become well organised by working upon itself and living in conformity with the Craft discipline. They are the fruits of the spirit: the energies and good works that it gives off.

To each of these two groups of seven must be added the Immediate Past Master. This is an Office of silence and reflection, where all the other Offices are summed up. The total of the constitutional Officers (omitting Assistants) is therefore fifteen. That number is important and recurs many times in the course of Craft teaching.

Every office in the Lodge is duplicated, or has its complementary part. There are two Wardens, two Deacons, two Doorkeepers, while the other Officers form pairs or counterparts. The reason is that the mind, as figured by the Lodge, is a field of interplay between the Spiritual and the Material, and its powers are double, acting upwards or downwards, actively or passively, as your Will directs.

All the Officers, like the non-official Brethren, are deemed to be in a state of perpetual watchfulness and obedience to their superiors. For they are all servants of the Master Principle, and the Master in turn is the servant of the Spirit above him.

The Master and Wardens use Gavels, not only as the emblem of power, but to illustrate how the vibrations of the Spirit pulse into the mind to stimulate and awaken it. What the superior light and wisdom of the Spirit knows to be necessary, and decrees to be done, must penetrate into and be obeyed by the lower nature. Therefore, when the Master Principle knocks, the command is repeated by the Wardens and made to reverberate through the entire Lodge. The knocks given by the Tyler are the converse of those given by the three Chairs; they represent the vibratory impulses of the lower nature beating upon the mind from without; whereas the knocks from the Chairs are those of the higher self, beating upon it from within. The mind is thus a field of vibratory activity, subject to competing claims from above it and below it. At each of its poles there is something which stands at the door and knocks, and each of us is free to determine which knocks we shall respond to.

The Deacons carry Wands. The Wand, is held over a Candidate's head at certain moments to signify the transmission of light and wisdom from above into his/her mind and lower nature. It is a symbolic conducting rod transmitting the current of the Spirit into the Candidate's bodily organism.

The Doorkeepers are armed with swords, emblems of the power of the Spirit to defend and control the lower nature of the human while labouring at the task of self-perfecting. The Masons engaged in rebuilding the wall of Jerusalem are described as labouring with a trowel in their hand and a sword upon their thigh; the former a constructive Tool for the work of up-building the mind; the latter a destructive weapon for combating the contrary tendencies of the flesh.

## A Progressive Science

Masonry is a progressive science because each of these Offices has its own unique lessons to teach the Master Elect. You first experience each of the three steps as a Candidate. You begin as a hoodwinked and tethered seeker after light, entering the Lodge but unable to see the light within it. You progress to study the hidden mysteries of nature and science with your eyes open in a fully illuminated Lodge of helpers. Then you and the Lodge both travel through the Valley of the Shadow of Death together: you to die, and the Officers of the Lodge to kill you, before you are raised to meet the Worshipful Master in the faint rays of the Bright Morning Star. Now, having been taken as far as the Lodge can take you as an individual, you have to join with the Lodge to learn the other side of knowledge. You will first Tyle the Lodge and challenge the Candidates. You will move on to hold the dagger to their naked left breasts. You will become the Younger Deacon and guide the newcomer, you will move to become the Elder Deacon and guide the Fellows on the paths of nature and science. You will become the Junior Warden and sit in the sunlight of knowledge, where you will call the brethren from refreshment to labour, and from labour to refreshment, as the work of the Lodge dictates. As you grow in understanding you will move to the rational West, where you will close the Lodge at the awful hour of disappearing light and will see that all have their due. Then you will move to the light of the East where you will employ and instruct your brethren in the Art of Freemasonry, and now will learn not only what it is like to be murdered but how to strike the fatal blow which lays your Brother dead in his grave. Finally you reach the quiet office of Immediate Past Master, where you sit in silence and reflect on what you have learned. Only now are you properly prepared to become a Real Initiate, rather than just a Master Mason in name.

In each of these offices you exist as a separate individual but you learn to combine into unity with your brethren, to form a Lodge. But as you do, you also realise that each of us is also an entire Lodge within him/herself; a composite assembly of many (not always harmonious) elements, needing to be organised, wrought into due form, and made perfect for the Great Architect's use.

By the help of our united work in the Lodge, we learn how to achieve this task and rule as Masters over ourselves.

To summarise, the seven Officers typify the following sevenfold parts of the human mind which must all work together to form a balanced and harmonious Master of the Craft:

| | |
|---|---|
| Worshipful Master | Spirit |
| Senior Warden | Mind |
| Junior Warden | Outer Personality |
| Senior Deacon | The link between Spirit and Mind |
| Junior Deacon | The link between Mind and Outer Personality |
| Inner Guard | The inner sense-nature (astral) |
| Outer Guard | The outer sense-nature (physical) |

Let me explain how a lodge functions by telling you a parable told by Walter Wilmshurst:

A man was seen loitering and apparently idle in a lonely district. He was asked what he was doing there. He replied that he was building a temple at a city many leagues away.

'Do you think it necessary,' he said 'for me to be there in person and working physically? Others are doing that who know nothing of me, but who are unconsciously influenced by the directive control of my thought and will as expressed through my plans and tracing boards.'

That man was a Master Mason who understood the working tools of an Initiate.

It is a useful Masonic exercise to think out clearly and in detail how that man made use of the Working Tools, and to realise that the Great Architect has built and sustains the universe upon the same principles. You are unlikely to reach a solution all at once, but persistent thought upon the subject opens out the mind.

The scientific inventions of our day are harbingers of greater truths yet to be learned. We have latent mental faculties in us, which the Craft teaches us to harness. Masonic Science and its understanding of the spiritual building-principle and the use of Working Tools to mould the spirit are of vital worth. They are the heritage of each Mason individually, and, through us, a benefit to the world.

May you all learn how to tyle the door of your Soul, to see that none but Masonic elements are present in it, and then to open the Perfect Lodge of your own being to your Centre, and so qualify yourself for those Greater Mysteries for which the lesser ones of our Craft are the necessary preparative.

This book has looked at the spiritual lessons of the Craft, trying to separate them from the mass of outward moral teaching within which they are deliberately veiled. I have written of many philosophic secrets. Some may startle you, or even offend you, until you learn to receive their hidden wisdom with the simple vision of a child.

But if you follow the discipline and industry of our Masonic system, you will become conscious of the Blazing Star rising at your centre. Its self-convincing light will disclose to you all that now lies secret and unexplained, enabling you to grow and develop. I wish you well in that endeavour.

# THE REAL INITIATE

*Although it is not part of the main theme of this book I felt it was important to discuss the origins and practical aspects of some the ideas I have ventured to lay before you, my Brethren and Sistren of The Craft. Hopefully this Afterword will afford some extra depth, background and practical tips to enable you work some of the ideas into your daily steps in Masonic Knowledge.*

The process of Initiation is one of regeneration. It means developing your inmost essence, first to birth and then to full growth. This involves a rejection and mystical death of all the lower principles that obstruct your growth. This path is traced through our three Degrees:

The first stage involves refining your gross sense-nature, killing your desire for material attractions and developing indifference to the allure of the outer world.

The second involves disciplining and clarifying your mind till it becomes pure and strong enough to respond to a spiritual order of life and wisdom. This is why in our Second Degree the discovery of a sacred symbol in the centre of the building shows a first glimpse of your personal centre. This knowledge is followed by a desire to wipe from your heart all obstacles to complete union with this Centre.

The third stage, the last and greatest trial, involves the voluntary death of your sense of ego and separation from the universal life-essence. As your limited personal ego dies, you become conscious of a Bright Morning Star within you, illuminating your mental horizon.

This is the great secret of Masonry: by instruction and discipline each of us can achieve conscious realisation of the unity of our Centre.

But why is such a theory a Secret Science? It is because it can only be understood as personal experience. The experience must be prepared for in secret, be realised in secret, and it remains incomprehensible and incommunicable to anyone who has not lived it. It is as mysterious as the redness of red or the feeling of love.

Masonry leaves you free to follow your own religion, in the sure knowledge that every religion leads ultimately to one Centre. It is a preparation for what can be realised in its fullness only by Initiation.

Therefore Masonry is not anti-religious, but super-sectarian. It is directed to secrets and mysteries of Being that popular religion does not address. It is ontological and philosophic, but not theological. Indeed it avoids all theologies, and so steers clear of all creeds and dogmas – save one.

In its Constitutions Masonry posits a sole dogma – belief in a form of Supreme Being. It wisely leaves that dogma unexplained and to be interpreted by you according to your lights. Nonetheless, its acceptance is a prerequisite for membership of the Order.

Religious thought, ideas of deity and the basic order of the cosmos, have travelled a long way since the time when the matters I am speaking of could never be breathed outside Temples of Initiation for fear of clashing with popular religion. But a need for disciplined instruction and Initiation into the Secrets and Mysteries of Being exists for all of us as much as it ever did in antiquity. We in the Craft possess an advantage over those who are not in it. If we rightly interpret and use it, we have in our Order a specialised system of guidance upon the path that leads to eternal truth.

Let us now consider what self-knowledge and realisation of the basic essence of our being is taught by our system.

## THE CONSCIOUSNESS OF THE INITIATE

The state of consciousness you achieve as an Initiate, what you know when you perceive the Centre, is known as cosmic consciousness. It is a state of awareness that has been much studied.

One of the first investigators to look at this topic was Dr Maurice Bucke, author of *Cosmic Consciousness: A Study in the Evolution of the Human Mind* (1901). More recently brain scan studies of meditating monks and nuns have shown it to be a real state of the brain. (For further discussion of this, see my book *Turning the Hiram Key*.)

In his book Bucke describes the sensations he felt when he first knew cosmic consciousness, an incident that led him to change his mental and spiritual attitude. It occurred in the early spring of his thirty-sixth year. He and two friends had spent the evening reading Wordsworth, Shelley, Keats, Browning and Whitman. They parted at midnight, and he had a long drive in a hansom cab through the city of London. His mind, deeply under the influence of the ideas, images and emotions called up by the reading and talk of the evening, was calm and peaceful. He was in a state of quiet, almost passive, enjoyment.

All at once, without any warning, he felt himself wrapped in a flame-coloured cloud. For an instant he thought the city was on fire. Then he realised that the light was within him. He felt a sense of exultation. It was a feeling of vast joy, along with complete intellectual insight. Into his brain streamed a lightning-flash of the splendour that ever after lightened his life. He said that 'upon his heart fell one drop of Brahmin Bliss, leaving thenceforward for always an aftertaste of heaven'.

Bucke claimed that in that unexpected moment of insight, he learned many things:

The Cosmos is not dead matter but a living presence.

The spirit of man is immortal.

The universe is built and ordered under the rule of a sacred law.

All things work together for the good of each and all.

The foundation principle of the world is what we call love.

The happiness of everyone is certain in the long run.

And he claimed he learned more in the few seconds that the illumination lasted than in many previous years of study.

And he learned much that no study could ever have taught.

This experience altered his whole outlook on life. But others have reported it, and in its purer forms it has certain characteristics. If you are affected, you realise as never before the oneness of the universe. You see yourself as part and parcel of this unity and sense in yourself the expression of a single conscious life. At the moment of the experience you realise the separateness of the ego and the non-ego. The distinction between the knower and the known, entirely disappears. You know the cosmos with a certainty that no argument or evidence can strengthen or shake. Jesus presumably had this experience on the Mount of Transfiguration, and the Buddha writes as if he was familiar with it: for instance, in his telling of how he attained this enlightenment under the Bodhi tree.

Among earlier mystics who had similar experiences St Paul is probably the most familiar. His first such experience was on the road to Damascus, when he was converted to Christianity and had a vision of the Christ, seeing a great light that had the effect of blinding him for some days afterwards. The other was many years later, when he was caught up into the Third Heaven and heard, as he says, unspeakable words that it is not lawful for a man to utter.

The seeing of this great light is a phenomenon that is recorded again and again in ancient records. We can associate these experiences with beatific vision. This comes more often to the religious devotee rather than the mystical philosopher but is a phase of the same experience. It may be that the beatific vision is in the nature of a realisation of the Higher Self in man, while cosmic consciousness is an intuitive perception of the essential oneness of universal consciousness.

According to how your mind is predisposed by your past life and spiritual outlook, so do you attain either a religious, a secular or a Masonic form of this awareness.

The most noteworthy records from early days, outside those of a specifically religious character, are those of the great mystical philosopher Plotinus (204–270 CE), whose philosophical training and ascetic life made him a favourable subject for this experience. His ideas about the true inwardness of the cosmic scheme are beautifully expressed in the following passage:

> There is a raying out of all orders of existence, an external emanation from the ineffable One. There is again a returning impulse, drawing all upwards and inwards towards the centre from whence all came. Love, as Plato in the *Symposium* beautifully says, is the child of poverty and plenty. In the amorous quest of the soul after the Good lies the painful sense of fall and deprivation. But that love is blessing, is salvation, is our guardian genius; without it the centrifugal law would overpower us and sweep our souls out far from their source toward the cold extremities of the material and the manifold. The wise man recognises the idea of the Good within him. This he develops by withdrawal into the place of his soul. He who does not understand how the soul contains the beautiful within itself, seeks to realise beauty without, by laborious production. His aim should rather be to concentrate and simplify, and so to expand his being; instead of going out into the manifold, to forsake it for the One, and so to float upwards towards the divine fount of being whose stream flows within him.

He asks how we can know the infinite, and replies that it cannot be known by reason. It can only be found by entering into a state in which man has his finite sense no longer, and in which the divine essence is communicated to him. This, he says, is ecstasy, and clearly by this expression, 'ecstasy' means standing outside oneself. This is the phenomenon we have met before that Burke called cosmic consciousness.

He adds, 'When you thus cease to be finite, you become one with the infinite.' This sublime condition is not of permanent duration and only now and then can it be enjoyed: 'I myself have realised it but three times as yet.' And he goes on to inform us that 'all that tends to purify and elevate the mind will assist us in this attainment, and will facilitate the approach and recurrence of these happy intervals.'

Plotinus offers a philosophical justification for this experience. External objects, he tells us, present us only with appearances. The problem of true knowledge, on the other hand, deals with the reality that exists behind these appearances. It follows that the truth is not to be investigated as something that is external to us, and so only imperfectly known. It actually is within us. Therefore, he maintains, that 'Truth is not the agreement of our apprehension of an external object with the object itself, but it is the agreement of the mind with itself'.

Hence, he contends, knowledge has three degrees: opinions, science and illumination. The instrument of the first is sense, of the second dialectic, and of the third intuition. This third is the absolute knowledge, founded on the identity of the mind knowing with the object known.

Between the post classical times of Plotinus and the later Middle Ages we have little evidence bearing on the phenomenon of cosmic consciousness. But then many experiences are recorded, with greater or less historical truth, of the Catholic saints of the period. Conspicuous among them are John Yepes, better known as St John of the Cross, and St Teresa, both of whom lived in the sixteenth century CE.

St John of the Cross was born in 1542 and died in 1591. At the age of twenty-one he became a Carmelite friar. In 1578 he was imprisoned for some months for practices of a kind regarded as unorthodox by the ecclesiastical authorities, and it was during this period that he had the mysterious psychic experience that Bucke identified as cosmic consciousness.

His translator, David Lewis, gives this account of it

His cell became filled with light seen by the bodily eye.
One night the friar who kept him went as usual to see that
his prisoner was safe and witnessed the heavenly light with
which the cell was flooded. He did not stop to consider it,
but hurried to the prior, thinking that some one in the
house had keys to open the doors of the prison. The prior,
with two members of the order, went at once to the
prison, but on his entering the room through which the
prison was approached, the light vanished. The prior,
however, entered the cell, and, finding it dark, opened the
lantern with which he had provided himself, and asked the
prisoner who had given him the light. St John answered
him, and said that no one in the house had done so, that no
one could do it, and that there was neither candle nor
lamp in the cell. The prior made no reply and went away,
thinking that the gaoler had made a mistake.

St John, at a later time, told one of his brethren that the
heavenly light, which God so mercifully sent him, lasted the
night through, and that it filled his soul with joy and made
the night pass away as if it were but a moment. When his
imprisonment was drawing to its close he heard our Lord
say to him, as it were out of the soft light that was around
him, 'John, I am here; be not afraid; I will set thee free.' A
few moments later, while making his escape from the
prison of the monastery, it is said that he had a repetition
of the experience, as follows:

He saw a wonderful light, out of which came a voice,
'Follow me.' He followed, and the light moved before him
towards the wall that was on the bank, and then, he knew
not how, he found himself on the summit of it without
effort or fatigue. He descended into the street, and then the
light vanished. So brilliant was it, that for two or three days
afterwards, so he confessed at a later time, his eyes were
weak, as if he had been looking at the sun in its strength.

Elsewhere John Yepes refers to his own spiritual experiences in language that suggests they were similar in character to those already mentioned. But his language is vague and unclear; he says that his description of his experience 'relates to matters so interior and spiritual as to baffle the powers of language.'

> All I say falls far short of that which passes in this intimate
> union of powers of the soul with God.... I stood enraptured
> in ecstasy beside myself, and in every sense no sense
> remained. My spirit was endowed with understanding,
> understanding not, all knowledge transcending.... He who
> really ascends so high annihilates himself, and all his
> previous knowledge seems ever less and less.

St Teresa's mystical experiences were manifold. They included the stigmata, levitation, clairvoyance, clairaudience, etc. But she also had an experience that she terms the 'orison of union,' which corresponds closely by its description to cosmic consciousness. This is how she described it.

> In this orison of union, the soul is fully awake as regards
> God, but wholly asleep as regards things of this world, and
> in respect of herself. During the short time the union lasts
> she is as it were deprived of every feeling, and even if she
> would she could not think of any single thing. Thus she
> needs to employ no artifice in order to assist the use of her
> understanding. In short, she is utterly dead to the things of
> the world, and lives solely in God.... Thus does God when
> He raises the soul to union with Himself suspend the natural
> action of all faculties. But this time is always short, and it
> seems even shorter than it is. God establishes Himself in the
> interior of this soul in such a way that when she returns to
> herself it is wholly impossible for her to doubt that she has
> been in God and God in her. This truth remains so strongly
> impressed on her that even though many years should pass
> without the condition returning, she can neither forget the

favour she received nor doubt of its reality. If you ask how it is possible that the soul can see and understand that she has been in God, since during the union she has neither sight nor understanding, I reply that she does not see it then, but that she sees it clearly later, after she has returned to herself, not by any vision but by a certitude which abides with her and which God alone can give her.

Of the same experience on another occasion, she recounts how one day it was granted to her to perceive in one instant how all things are seen and contained in God.

I did not perceive them in their proper form, and nevertheless the view I had of them was of a sovereign clearness and has remained vividly impressed upon my soul. This view was so subtle and delicate that the understanding cannot grasp it.

Jacob Boehme (1575–1624) is another classic example of a man who had this experience. His first illumination occurred in 1600, when he was twenty-five. He had a further and more vivid experience ten years later. This is how he described his first experience:

Sitting one day in his room my eyes fell upon a burnished pewter dish, which reflected the sunshine with such marvellous splendour that I fell into an inward ecstasy, and it seemed to me as if I could now look into the principles and deepest foundation of things. I believed that it was only a fancy, and in order to banish it from my mind I went out upon the green. But here I gazed into the very heart of things, the very herbs and grass, and that actual nature harmonised with what I had inwardly seen. I said nothing to anyone, but praised and thanked God in silence. I continued in the honest practice of my craft, was attentive to my domestic affairs, and was on terms of good will with all men.

Of his complete illumination ten years later he says:

> The gate was opened to me that in one quarter of an hour
> I saw and knew more than if I had been many years
> together at a university, at which I exceedingly admired
> and thereupon turned my praise to God for it. For I saw
> and knew the being of all things. . . . And I saw and knew
> the whole working essence, in the evil and the good and
> the original and the existence of each of them; and
> likewise how the fruit-bearing womb of eternity brought
> forth. So that I not only did greatly wonder at it but did
> also exceedingly rejoice.

In more recent times James Allen, the author of *From Poverty to Power* (1901) and *As a Man Thinketh* (1902) wrote about the experience of cosmic consciousness. So did Edward Carpenter, the author of *Towards Democracy* (1883), who described his experience in a letter to Dr Bucke:

> I really do not feel that I can tell you anything without
> falsifying and obscuring the matter. I had no experience of
> physical light in this relation. The perception seems to be
> one in which all the senses unite into one sense, in which
> you become the object, but this is unintelligible mentally
> speaking. I do not think the matter can be defined as yet, but
> I do not know that there is any harm in writing about it.

Elsewhere, in *Civilisation: Its Cause and Cure* (1889), he writes more definitely on the subject:

> There is in every man a local consciousness connected
> with his quite external body. That we know. Is there not
> also in every man the making of a universal consciousness?
> That there are in us phases of consciousness that transcend
> the limit of the bodily senses is a matter of daily
> experience. That we perceive and know things that are not

conveyed to us by the bodily eyes and heard by our bodily
ears is certain. That there arise in us waves of
consciousness from those around us, from the people, the
race to which we belong, is also certain. May there not
then be in us the makings of a perception and knowledge
which shall not be relative to this body which is here and
now, but which shall be good for all time and everywhere?
Does there not exist in truth, as we have already hinted, an
inner illumination, of which what we call light in the outer
world is the partial expression and manifestation, by which
we can ultimately see things as they are, beholding all
creation, not by any local act of perception, but by a
cosmical intuition and prescience, identifying ourselves
with what we see? Does there not exist a perfected sense
of hearing, as of the morning stars singing together, an
understanding of the words that are spoken all through the
universe, the hidden meaning of all things, a profound and
far-pervading sense of which our ordinary sense of sound
is only the first novitiate and intuition?

Carpenter refers elsewhere to 'that inner vision which transcends
sight as far as sight transcends touch' and to 'a consciousness in
which the contrast between the ego and the external world and the
distinction between subject and object fall away.' These are surely
the words of one who has undergone the experience of cosmic
consciousness. Carpenter, however, is careful to warn us that we are
not to suppose that people who have this experience are in any way
to be regarded as infallible as to its exact meaning. 'In many cases
indeed,' he remarks, 'the very novelty and strangeness of the
experience may give rise to phantasmal trains of delusive
speculation.'

Trying to interpret this mystery he says that the whole body is,
as it were, one organ of the cosmic consciousness. 'To attain this
latter one must have the power of knowing oneself separate from
the body, of passing into a state of ecstasy, in fact. Without this,
cosmic consciousness cannot be experienced.'

It is useful that Carpenter wrote so definitely of the matter and adopted such an impersonal tone. Often those who have experienced this state have been too reserved about their spiritual experiences and too moved by it to exercise their critical faculty to give us a satisfactory explanation of the phenomenon.

The well-known practice of yoga offers a training that lends itself naturally to producing such phenomena. Its goal is the attainment of *samadhi*, a state identical with that known in the West as cosmic consciousness.

None of these writers were Freemasons or knew anything of the spiritual teaching of the Craft, yet they all describe the state of being that we Masons strive for in our journey from West to East. This journey, whose route is shown in the Tracing Board of the Centre, is a journey through darkness, passing through the invisible light of the Centre.

In our own day, writer and philosopher Colin Wilson has studied this state of mind. He calls it Peak Experience and tells how it leads to creativity in both the arts and the sciences. In his autobiography *Dreaming to Some Purpose* (2004), he describes techniques for achieving it.

## How Can You Make Darkness Visible in Your Lodge?

The popular appeal of Masonry and the tendency of its members to be content with its surface attraction have resulted in the original idea of a Lodge becoming neglected. The popular idea of a successful Lodge is one that has many members, works degrees at every meeting, has loads of candidates, and a strong social programme.

These social interactions have their worth, but the original idea of a Lodge was quite different: it was conceived as a small community devoting itself in privacy to corporate work of a philosophical nature. This was for the intellectual development and spiritual perfecting of its members; social amenities should be secondary. It is desirable to revive these ideas if you want to return to the spiritual dimension of the Craft. Its real purpose is to provide a model of the inner workings of the human mind and so provide a group to assist nominal Initiates realise their full potential as they progressively learn to know themselves.

The strength and worth of a Lodge does not depend upon numbers and popular attractions. It rests on the quality of the corporate life of its members. It depends on their united and consistent co-operation towards a common ideal. Its success relies on their ability to form a group consciousness. To achieve these ends there are two methods.

1. A shared rule of personal life, and

2. A way by which all members can constitute a group-mind.

The Craft is not a monastic community, it is a discipline of the secret that is adapted to people who live in the real world, and who discharge domestic and secular duties. It does not call upon you to follow any uniform rule of life, such as is followed in an enclosed order. It leaves you to live your life in your own fashion but helps you acquire a unique way to harmonise your outward and inward lives.

It does, however, make definite provision in three respects. These guidelines constitute a rule of life.

1. It emphasises continual obedience to Moral Law.

2. It calls for daily progress in Masonic Science by the use of some form of helpful study, reflection or meditative practice, adapted to your taste and temperament.

3. It provides the symbolism of the Working Tools and the Tracing Boards for daily contemplation and reflection.

If you wish to become a Real Initiate you should pay attention to these points. This especially applies to the personal use of the symbolic Working Tools and Tracing Boards, which cannot be too closely or too often pondered upon and applied.

## Forms of Masonic Meditation

### *Using Tracing Boards*

To develop this technique you can obtain small reproductions of the four Tracing Boards and use them as a focus for meditation. My own method is to set aside fifteen minutes or so (I use a small electronic timer so I don't have to clock-watch), usually in the late evening when the household is quiet. I lower the room lights and just have a single light illuminating the Tracing Board of the Degree I wish to reflect on. To remind you, the First-Degree Tracing Board is about emotional control, the Second about developing the intellect, the Third about controlling the Ego, and the Tracing Board of the Centre is about the Masonic Plan for the creation of a perfected Temple of Humanity. Each of the Tracing Boards has an associated posture and sign, which I use whilst reflecting on the Board. My aim is to maintain my body in perfect stillness, whilst holding the correct posture.

In this form of meditation I do not try to suppress all thoughts, I simply focus on the images on the Tracing Board, maintain the posture of the Degree and let my thoughts about those images go where they will.

### *Using the Mason Word*

In this form of meditation I again set aside thirty minutes or so in a quiet, usually darkened room. Again, I use a timer

I sit in a comfortable but upright chair and systematically relax my body. Working from my feet up to my neck. I stretch and settle each limb and appendage in turn before closing my eyes and slowly repeating the Mason Word silently in my mind. I breathe in as I say the first part, syllable by syllable, ... pause with my breath held in for a few seconds, ... then exhale slowly whilst saying the second part of the Mason Word in the silent Centre of my mind. Finally I pause for a few seconds with my lungs empty before beginning the whole cycle again.

As a basic discipline I switch between meditating on each of the Tracing Boards and meditating using the Mason Word method. In this way I reflect on the meanings of the Degrees, with each Board and then on the darkness visible at the Centre using the Mantra of the Mason Word. Using these methods I try to make my daily advancement in Masonic knowledge. By practising these simple and elementary workings of the Craft, I hope to prepare my mind for its more advanced and concealed teachings, which will only reveal themselves through the work of the group-mind of the lodge.

## THE MEDITATING LODGE

As a member of a lodge you value that membership. But you are asked to do more than merely have a sentimental attachment to it. You are invited to co-operate actively and systematically with every other Brother in a concerted effort to realise your Lodge as an organic unity of minds. It should be more than a temporary association of persons.

Physically we are separate individuals. We live in different places. We have our personal responsibilities and duties. But mentally you should learn to become a Free Mason and an active member of your Lodge. By that I mean that you should assert the freedom of your spirit to rise above the limitations of separateness and distance. You can agree with your brethren to meet at the common Centre, and there, literally and Masonically, build yourselves into a mental community or group-mind. This is the real purpose of the Masonic building art.

Let your Lodge Room or Temple be your psychological meeting-place. Every day, let each of you make a point of projecting your will, for at least a few moments, in an effort to realise your corporate unity with one another.

Following the precedent of our Grand Master Hiram Abif at the hour of high-twelve, every day at noon banish every other concern from your thoughts and try to visualise yourself and your fellow-members gathered together in Lodge, in peace, concord and harmony with each other. It is useful if all agree to recite the same piece of ritual together to form a focal point.

If the Brethren will do this conscientiously and regularly, the following results will ensue:

1. In a mental but real sense the Lodge will be meeting every day, not just at infrequent intervals.

2. The practice will greatly contribute to harmony of thought, unity and concentration of purpose on occasions when you meet physically.

3. The Lodge Room will increasingly fulfil the purpose for which its Consecration Rite was held. It will form a focus point and storage place for the members' collective thought and aspiration.

You should contribute your daily quota to this concerted work at the Lodge Room, and you may regard it is part of the daily Masonic labour to which you are committed. This is a real use of the 24-inch gauge, whether it is thought of as labour, refreshment or prayer. You will probably find it comprehends all three categories.

I encourage you not to give up on this effort simply because it may feel futile or fanciful. You may experience no benefit from it at first. But if you persist you will experience results. Remember, no one can enter the Lodge without first meeting opposition and giving the proper knocks. In this higher sense of seeking to enter the Lodge you may meet with barriers of inertia, diffidence or unbelief within yourself. These will only give way when you apply knocks of resolute effort to them.

Likewise do not suppose that your contribution to this work is too feeble to be worth making. The very desire to collaborate is itself a contribution. The more you develop that desire by practice, the greater will be your contribution. In meeting upon the level of a common aim, the widow's mite is of equal value to the rich man's gold.

If you are tempted to give it a miss, because of either indolence or pressure of work, then reflect that by not doing your part you hamper the collective effort. Group work requires the loyal assistance of the whole community. Loose or missing stones imperil a building.

If you cannot observe the practice precisely at noon, perform it as near to that time as you can. (You can, of course, repeat it at other times of the day, and as often as you want, in addition to the appointment at High Twelve.)

Reflect that the stronger the group mind becomes, the stronger the mystic tie is knitted. You will benefit by reaction from this increase in strength. As vapour rises from the ground and forms a cloud, from which rain falls to replenish the earth, so from the collective thought and aspiration of the lodge there will be a return current of ideas upon each Brother contributing to it. In this, as in other regions of nature, action and reaction are equal and opposite. By drawing from the common pool of thought energy, the weaker and less efficient contributor becomes enriched by the contributions of the more capable ones, and so is gradually raised to equality with them.